COPAN

Jürgen
Partenheimer

COPAN

Diario Paulistano
São Paulo Tagebuch
São Paulo Diary

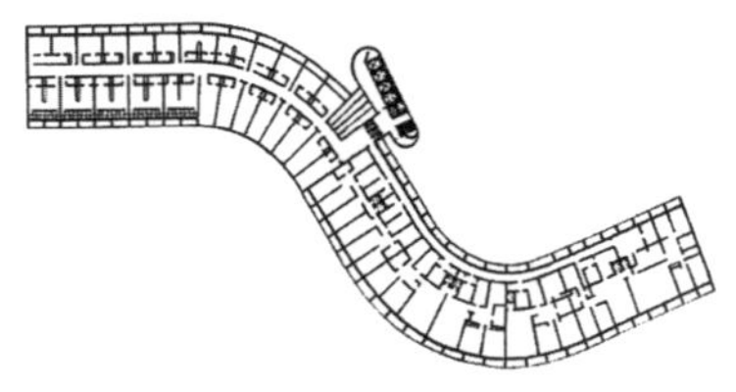

21. 3. – 18. 4. 2005

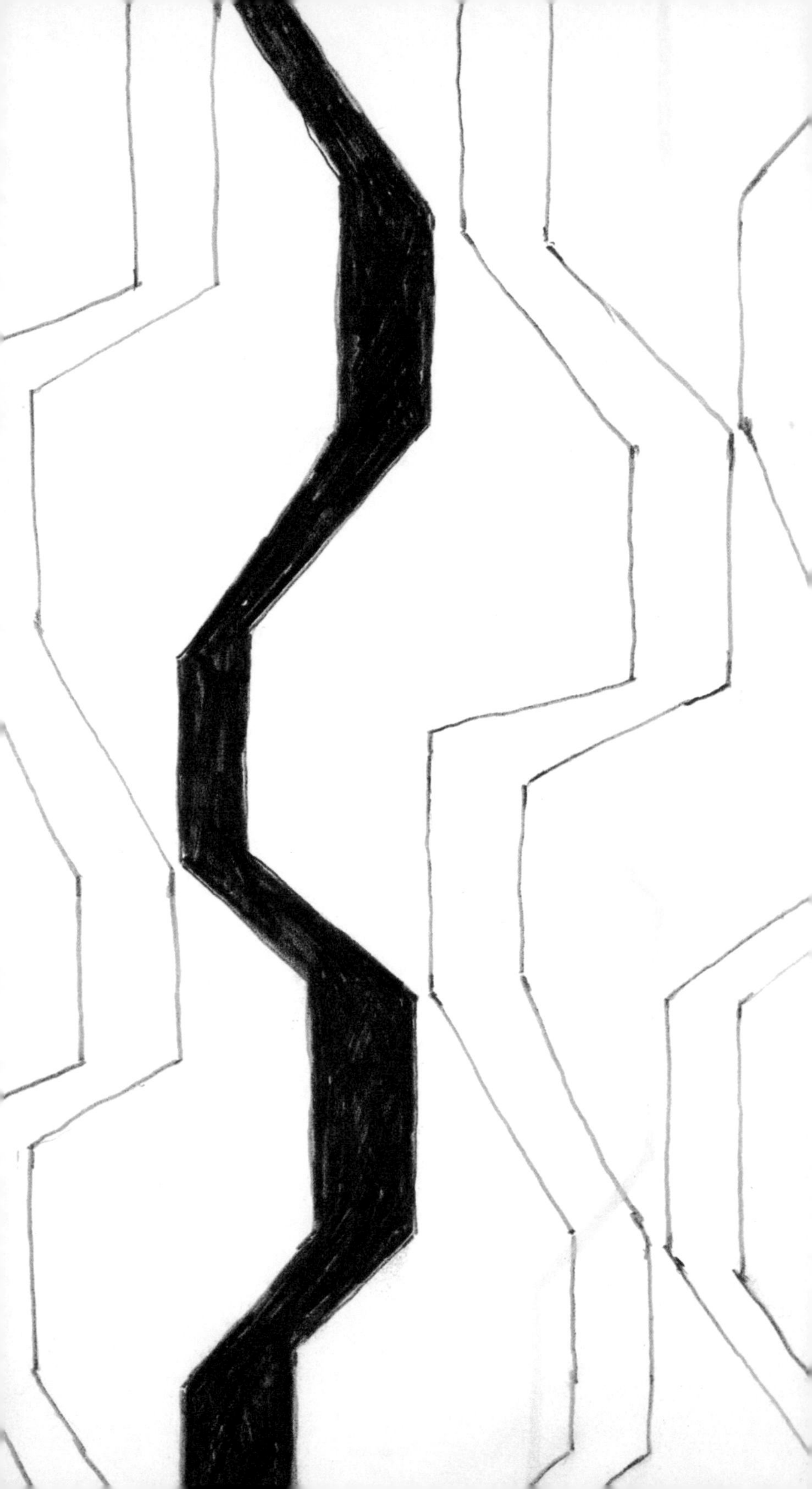

COPAN

São Paulo

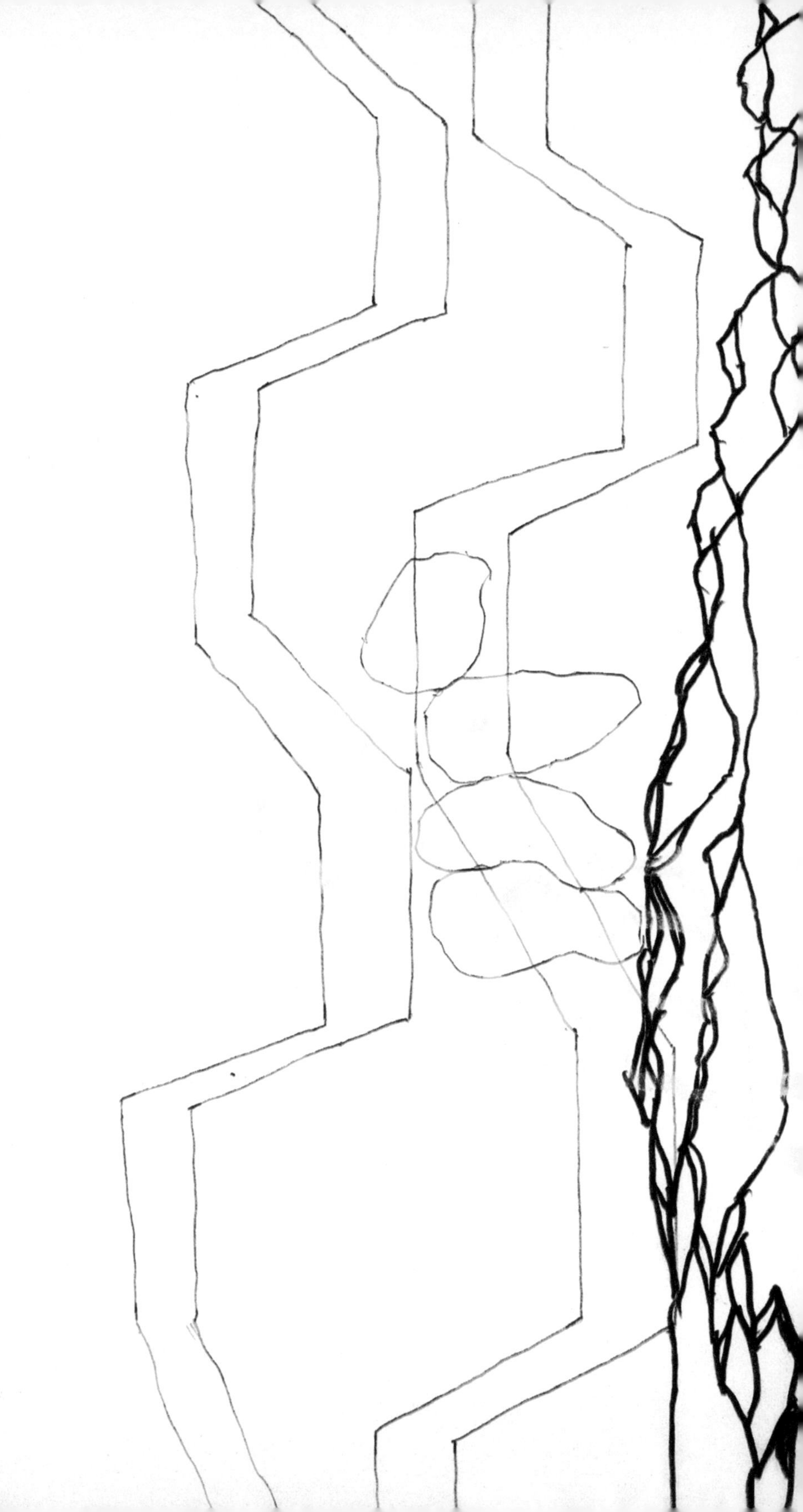

21/22/23/24/25/26/27/28/29/

30/31/01/02/03/04/05/06/07/

08/09/10/11/12/13/14/15/16/

17/18/

"Because it is by no means a matter of awareness, but of vision, of simply seeing. Simply!"
Samuel Beckett

»*Denn es geht hier nicht darum, sich etwas bewusst zu machen, sondern darum, ein inneres Bild einzufangen, um eine Innenaufnahme kurzum. Kurzum!*«

Samuel Beckett

01 A pall of heavy, sultry air, laden with petrol fumes, smothers the city.

01 Schwere, feuchtwarme Benzinluft liegt über der Stadt.

02 I live in the concave part of the Copan's wave. My apartment measures 567 x 670 cm, which is slightly more than 34 square meters of living space. The height of the ceiling is 279 cm. Although the window on the building's façade fills the entire width and height of the room, it does not afford a full view, but restricts, at a height of one meter, my vision to a kind of full-width viewing panel measuring only 90 cm in height and 670 cm in length. From the parquet floor to a height of one meter, the window is glazed with a thick pane of translucent yet opaque safety glass with a finely ribbed, bubbly structure. Leathery to the touch, like the skin of a lizard, the window arches across the room and its tiny, locked-in bubbles seem to move about like specimens of viral cultures under the microscope – a gigantic, frozen culture cast in slabs of gelatin.

In the upper third of the window heavy concrete slabs, spaced 90 cm apart, divide the façade of the building into strips and restrict my vision horizontally. Thus the entire front is clad in a concrete structure of horizontal elements, each one of which is anchored in the ends of the right-hand and left-hand walls of each dwelling unit with a clearance of 28 cm. These concrete elements take the form of 16 cm thick ledges 146 cm deep, and, like a table in front of a window, extend one's sensation of space beyond the actual space of the living room. Like the slats of a louvered shutter the ledges are let into two slender concrete uprights 105 cm deep, which stand flush with the right-hand and left-hand partition walls of the apartment units, thus heightening the impression of spatial expansion and at the

02 Ich lebe im konkaven Teil der Welle des Copan. Mein Apartment misst 567 x 670 cm, das sind etwas über 34 qm Wohnfläche. Die Deckenhöhe beträgt 279 cm. Zur Fassadenseite des Gebäudes nimmt eine Fensterfront die vollständige Breite und Höhe des Raumes ein, die jedoch keinen großflächigen Blick freigibt, sondern auf der Höhe von einem Meter über dem Boden nur ein 90 cm hohes und 670 cm breites Sichtband zulässt. Die Fläche des Fensters vom Parkettboden bis zur Höhe von einem Meter ist mit starkem, undurchsichtigem Sicherheitsglas von fein geriffelter Bläschenstruktur eingefasst. Ledrig wie die Haut einer Echse buckelt das Glas über die Fläche und die in ihm eingeschlossenen Bläschen scheinen sich zu bewegen wie das Bild einer Virenkultur unter dem Mikroskop – eine riesige gefrorene Kultur, deren gallertartige Masse in Gelatine Tafeln gegossen ist.

Im oberen Drittel der Fensterfront durchtrennen schwere Betonbänder den Blick horizontal und teilen so im Abstand von jeweils 90 cm die gesamte Fassade des Hauses in Streifen. Auf diese Weise ist der Fensterfläche eine Betonstruktur vorgeblendet, die in einer knappen Distanz von nur 28 cm in den rechten und linken Wandbegrenzungen jeder Wohneinheit in der Außenwand verankert ist. Diese vorgeblendeten Betonbänder sind 16 cm dick und liegen als Tafeln, 146 cm breit, wie ein Tisch vor dem Fenster und vertiefen das Raumgefühl über den tatsächlichen Wohnraum hinaus. Wie Lamellen sind die Bänder in schlanke, 26 cm starke vertikale Stützen eingelassen, die mit einer Breite von 105 cm bündig die begrenzenden Wände der Wohnung rechts und links abschließen und so den Ein-

same time confining one's vision. The feeling of living behind a lookout slot and experiencing the world through a very wide panorama box on an imaginary Cinemascope screen dominates both the mental and physical perception of every movement. Thus the height of the interior is divided horizontally by the external slabs into three distinct spaces.

When I am standing, my eye level is slightly below the upper dividing line, while the lower dividing line stretches out in front of me at navel level. A table top measuring 625 x 146 cm lies in front of my window on the 28th floor and repeats itself a thousand times over, downwards, upwards, to the right and to the left. My view of the world has a standardized format: ninety times six hundred and twenty-five centimeters.

I am sitting in the concave part of the wave, in one of those countless honeycomb cells, which, through the seemingly endless repetition of their form, turn the building's exterior into a gigantic structure of slatted latticework.

My desk stands in front of the façade window. My gaze rests on the table top formed by the concrete ledge before me, while above me hangs the plastered underside of the ledge that forms the ceiling of my panorama box. These two heavy, slightly inward-curving ledges of concrete dominate my gaze, as though they are the touchdown and launching ramp of vision. Aimless, purposeless tranquility takes over. The limits imposed by the panorama box seem to focus my perception, adjust my way of seeing, and spare me the vastness of infinity. Like blinkers, the uprights on either

druck der Erweiterung des Wohnraumes nach Außen betonen und gleichzeitig den Blick einengen. Das Gefühl hinter einem Sehschlitz zu leben und die Welt durch eine lang gestreckte Panorama-Box auf einer imaginären Filmleinwand zu erfahren dominiert physisch und psychisch die Wahrnehmung jeder Bewegung. So wird die Höhe des Wohnraumes nach Außen von den vor gelagerten Bändern in 3 horizontale Lichträume geteilt.

Im Stehen stößt die Augenhöhe leicht unter die obere Begrenzung des zweiten Bandes, und auf Bauchhöhe dehnt sich vor mir das erste Band in die Tiefe des Raumes. Eine Tischplatte von 625 x 146 cm liegt vor meinem Fenster im 28. Stock, und alle 90 cm wiederholt sich diese Form tausendfach nach oben, unten, rechts und links. Mein Blickfeld in die Welt hat Standardformat: neunzig mal sechshundertfünfundzwanzig Zentimeter.

Im konkaven Teil der Welle sitze ich in einer dieser unzähligen Waben, die das Gebäude nach Außen in der scheinbar unendlichen Vervielfältigung ihrer Form zu einem riesigen Lamellengitterwerk gestalten.

Mein Schreibtisch steht an der Fensterfassade des Zimmers. Der Blick legt sich auf die Tafelfläche des Betonbandes vor mir, und über mir hängt die verputzte Unterseite des nächsten Bandes als Decke meiner Sichtbox. Die leicht konkav gekrümmte, lastende Form drängt sich in den Blick wie eine Start- und Landebahn des Sehens. Absichtsloses, zielloses Ruhen stellt sich ein. Die Beschränkung der Sichtbox erscheint zugleich als eine Art der Fokussierung, sie richtet mich aus, erspart mir die uneingeschränkte Weite. Schützend leiten die Scheuklappen der

side shield the eye and gently guide my gaze into a cropped world, an expanse of space across the city to the horizon. And so the view moves gently southeast across the sea of houses bordered in the distance by mountain ridges. There the city eats its way into the slopes of the gently rising valleys and in many places the stony fields begin to swallow up the mountain forests like lava.

flachen Pfeilerflächen das Auge in eine Welt, die in der
Enge des Ausschnitts die Weite des Raumes über der Stadt
bis zum Horizont spannt. Der Blick gleitet südöstlich
über das Häusermeer, das in der Ferne von Bergrücken
eingefasst wird. Dort frisst sich die Stadt in die Hügel der
flach ansteigenden Täler und an manchen Stellen beginnt
das Steinfeld einen Teil der Bergwälder wie Lava zu ver-
schlucken.

03 I read through my first entry about the dimensions of the apartment, the tininess of which radiates a
remarkably beneficial generosity. Daily life is behind
me, behind my back, for at my desk in front of my lookout slot, in the safety of my bunker I do not sense the
crampedness of my living room, but rather experience
the ungraspable expanse of the world before me. Sea-
ted on the brink of reality, I begin to dream of possible
realities in which the observer remains a mirror of the
observed.

Stretching out before me lie vast fields of stone towers, the sprouting offshoot of the family towers of San
Gimignano, symbols of protection and power. Here,
eight hundred years later, it is the popularized extrava-
gance of rivalry and pretence. Fired by ambition for
prestige and control, the buildings soar skywards: hun-
dreds of thousands of times, the mysteriously anonymous clusters of dwelling machines repeat themselves, the irrational connection between them being
just a common yearning for status. How beautifully and
boundlessly they spread, these places of refuge and
symbols of mutual exploitation and dependence, like
hastily growing toxic fungi surfacing from the depths
with gargantuan deliberation and complete lack of
control.

The early morning sun is caught in the waves of the
towers. Unemotionally, mercilessly, it shines on their
bright concrete blades. Over the stony field the sky
stretches and the bright, low rising eastern light paints
the city in stripes. The crests of the highest buildings
parry the garish light off their sides, when suddenly

03 Ich lese den ersten Eintrag über die Raummaße der Wohnung, deren Enge eine merkwürdig wohltuende Großzügigkeit ausstrahlt. Das tägliche Leben liegt hinter mir, in meinem Rücken, da ich am Tisch vor meinem Sehschlitz wie in einem sicheren Bunker nicht die Enge des Standortes empfinde, sondern die nicht fassbare Ausdehnung der Welt vor mir erlebe. Vor dem Abgrund der Realität breitet sich der Traum möglicher Wirklichkeiten aus, in dem der Beobachter Spiegel des Beobachteten bleibt.

Vor mir liegen die weiten Felder einer aufgegangenen Saat steinerner Türme, Ableger der Geschlechtertürme von San Gimignano, Zeichen von Schutz und Macht. 800 Jahre später, hier, die Popularisierung der Extravaganz von Rivalität und Anspruch. Durch Ehrgeiz und Kontrolle inspiriert, treiben die Gebäude in die Höhe. Hunderttausendfach wiederholt sich die geheimnisvoll anonyme Gruppierung der Wohnmaschinen, deren irrationaler Zusammenhang in der Gemeinsamkeit der Sehnsucht nach Erfolg besteht, Zuflucht und Symbol gegenseitiger Ausbeutung und Abhängigkeit. Maßlos und schön dehnen sie sich aus, wie ein vergiftetes Myzel, das die Signale des Wachstums irritiert beschleunigt und aus der Tiefe unkontrolliert und gewollt wie ein Streich Gargantuas an die Oberfläche drängt.

In den Wogen der Türme fängt sich die frühe Morgensonne. Unbewegt und ohne Gnade bestrahlt sie die hellen Flächen der Betonhalme. Über dem Steinfeld streckt sich der Himmel, und das starke, flach aufgehende Ostlicht wirft die Sonne in Streifen in die Stadt. Die Kämme der höchsten Gebäude weisen das grelle Licht von ihren Flan-

some of them rise out of the grey veil of morning haze like silhouettes, stand out sharply in the cone of light and plunge the rest of the city into the semidarkness of a Dutch landscape, vanishing in banks of clouds on the distant horizon.

I am sitting behind the slats. The noise of the streets below, which I cannot see, is just as abstractly present as the air, and the movement of the cars between the houses in the distance is strangely static, like rows of moving targets in a shooting gallery, noiseless and anonymous. The cell in which I live, 28 stories above the ground, hidden by the slats, seems suspended in mid-air, detached from the world, isolated, completely disconnected from the countless dens above, below and on either side of me. With a feeling of emptiness I search about my room for the 18 million inhabitants of this city.

The expanding depth of the concrete ledges, which constantly perturb and manipulate me, and their narrow stratification before my eyes, which makes the room behind me grow in size, conveying the feeling that being able to stand upright is a privilege, are the sensitive expression of a way of thinking that is very close to nature. The slatted box in front of my window turns out to be a clever but callous fender against the sun's rays, a *brise soleil* that affords every dwelling cell the necessary shade and coolness. Behind these slats the inhabitants of the Copan Building are protected from the heat and light of the sun like the Mediterraneans in the narrow streets of their villages.

I am writing in a slightly dazed state following a sudden compulsion to do fifty knee-bends with out-

ken zurück – plötzlich erhebt sich ein Teil kulissenhaft aus dem grauen Schleier des Morgens, trennt sich scharf im Kegel des Lichtes und versenkt den Rest der Stadt in das Halbdunkel einer niederländischen Landschaft, die sich über dem Horizont in den Wolkenbändern verliert.

Ich sitze hinter den Lamellen. Der Lärm der Straßen unter mir, die ich nicht sehen kann, ist ebenso abstrakt gegenwärtig wie die Luft, und die Bewegung der Autos, die in weiter Ferne zwischen den Häusern wie auf einem Schießbudenstand aufgereiht merkwürdig statisch vorbeiziehen, ist lautlos, ohne Identität. Die Wabe, in der ich lebe, 28 Stockwerke über dem Boden, von den Lamellen verdeckt, erscheint mir suspendiert, außerhalb der Welt, ohne Zusammenhang und ohne jede Verbindung zu den unzähligen Zellen neben, über und unter mir. Menschenleer verpackt, suche ich die 18 Millionen Bewohner dieser Stadt in meinem Zimmer.

Die ausladende Tiefe der Betonbänder, die mich stetig bedrängen und manipulieren, die enge Schichtung vor meinen Augen, die den Raum hinter mir wachsen lässt und das Gefühl aufrechten Stehens als Privileg vermittelt, sind sensibler Ausdruck eines naturnahen Denkens. Die Lamellenbox vor meinem Fenster erweist sich als kluge, aber herzlose Konstruktion Licht abweisender Sonneneinstrahlung, eine ›brise soleil‹, die jeder Wohnzelle notwendigen Schatten und Kühle spendet. Hinter den Lamellenbändern leben die Menschen im Copan wie in den engen Gassen mediterraner Dörfer, vor dem Licht und der Hitze der Sonne geschützt.

Leicht benommen schreibe ich nach dem plötzlichen

stretched arms, triggered by the cool intelligence of these hovering ledges of concrete, each one of which is covered with 21,000 whitish grey mosaic tiles. They lie before me in broken lines on the launching ramp of my vision, of my leap into the city. I have counted them.

Registering one's observations is a kind of conquest, an appropriation of the unfamiliar, a plausible perception of architectonic causality for latitudes south of the equator – a mixed feeling of aloofness and restlessness comes over me. Perception leads to an emotional struggle between my self-chosen seclusion and my desire for a recognition of either the courage or the absurdity of my decision in favor of this city. Preserve anonymity, calmness – 'la vie dans les plis' – how did Henri Michaux come upon that image?

Can one be one's own narrator? Can anything be added to Pessoa's *Book of Disquiet* or Sartre's *Nausea* with the alarmingly beautiful clarity of the psychoanalysis of hopelessness as communication? It is the endless 'essential loneliness' – the soliloquy, the confession, the attempt at communication, aloof empathy, squandering as meticulous analysis – a wandering through the depths of fear and contempt for the world with the nonchalance of a flâneur. Senselessness, once formulated, disproves itself through the vastness of its professional communication, or is it about the fulfilled longing for objective detachment through the anonymous universality of the participating subjects? The flâneur pretends to stroll, but secretly, perhaps, it is the despair of having nothing to do that forces him to walk the streets with the self-imposed detachment of an observer.

Verlangen von 50 Kniebeugen mit gestreckten Armen, ausgelöst durch die kühle Intelligenz der schwebenden Betonflächen, die jeweils von 21.000 weißgrauen Mosaiksteinen überzogen sind. Vor mir auf meiner Blickrampe, über die ich in die Stadt springe, liegen die in gebrochenen Linien verlegten Steine, ich habe sie gezählt.

Die registrierende Beobachtung ist eine Form der Eroberung, eine Aneignung der Fremde, plausible Wahrnehmung architektonischer Kausalität für Breitengrade südlich des Äquators – Distanz stellt sich ein und gleichzeitige Unruhe. Die Wahrnehmung mündet in Emotion, es ist das Ringen zwischen selbst gewählter Zurückgezogenheit und ersehnter Aufmerksamkeit für den Mut oder die Absurdität der Entscheidung für die Stadt. Anonymität bewahren, Ruhe – ›la vie dans les plis‹ – wie kam Henri Michaux auf dieses Bild?

Kann man sein eigener Erzähler sein? Kann Pessoas *Buch der Unruhe* oder Sartres *Ekel* etwas hinzugefügt werden in der erschreckend schönen Klarheit der Psychoanalyse der Ausweglosigkeit als Kommunikation? Es ist die nicht endende ›wesentliche Einsamkeit‹ aller, der innere Monolog, Entwurf des Bekennens, Versuch der Mitteilung, distanzierte Empathie, Verschwendung als akribische Analyse – mit der gelassenen Heiterkeit eines Flaneurs in den Untiefen von Angst und Weltverachtung schlendern. Die formulierte Sinnlosigkeit widerlegt sich in der Auflagenhöhe ihrer qualifizierten Mitteilung, oder ist es die eingelöste Sehnsucht nach objektiver Distanz durch die anonyme Universalität der teilhabenden Subjekte? Der Flaneur gibt vor zu flanieren. Insgeheim mag

Helicopters buzz around like bees over the tall-stalked high-rise buildings, gingerly navigate their way to the landing pads of their hives, dive down between the towers, deposit their nectar and set off for new destinations.

The luxury of Sartre's nausea lay in the fact that it took hold of him in a café in pre-war France. What an idyllic place of melancholy, for it was there that the hesitant retreat from everyday life, with a filterless Gauloise and a glass of the notorious absinthe, became the literary tradition of modernism. It was there that the laws of unaccelerated time permitted the sensitive, contemplative perception of transience: "I very much like to pick up chestnuts, old rags and especially papers. It is pleasant to me to pick them up, to close my hand on them; with a little encouragement I would carry them to my mouth the way children do. [...] In summer or the beginning of autumn, you can find remnants of sun-baked newspapers in gardens, dry and fragile as dead leaves, so yellow you might think they had been washed with picric acid. In winter, some pages are pounded to pulp; crushed, stained, they return to the earth. Others quite new when covered with ice, all white, all throbbing, are like swans about to fly, but the earth has already caught them from below. They twist and tear themselves from the mud, only to be finally flattened out a little further on. It is good to pick up all that. Sometimes I simply feel them, looking at them closely; other times I tear them to hear their drawn-out crackling, or, if they are damp, I light them, not without difficulty; then I wipe my muddy hands on a wall or tree

ihn die Verzweiflung des Nichtstuns durch die Straßen treiben, gehetzt in die selbst auferlegte Distanz des Beobachters.

Wie Bienen schwirren die Hubschrauber über den langstieligen Hochhäusern, suchen behutsam navigierend die Landeplattform ihrer Bienenstöcke, tauchen ein zwischen den Türmen der Stadt, legen ihre Frucht ab und entfernen sich mit neuem Ziel.

Der Luxus von Sartres Ekel bestand darin, dass er ihn in einem Café im Frankreich der Vorkriegszeit ereilen konnte. Was für ein idyllischer Ort der Wehmut, an dem der zaghafte Rückzug aus dem Alltag literarische Tradition der Moderne wurde mit filterloser Gauloise und dem notorischen Glas Absinth. Dort erlaubten die Gesetze unbeschleunigter Zeit die zarte Wahrnehmung kontemplativer Vergänglichkeit: »Ich hebe gern Kastanien, alte Fetzen, vor allem Papierstückchen auf. Ich empfinde es angenehm, sie aufzunehmen, meine Hand über ihnen zu schließen; es fehlte nicht viel, und ich würde sie, wie es Kinder tun, an den Mund führen [...] Im Sommer oder zu Beginn des Herbstes findet man in den Anlagen Zeitungsfetzen, von der Sonne gedörrt, trocken und zerbrechlich wie tote Blätter und so gelb als wären sie mit einer Säure imprägniert. Andere Blätter wiederum kehren im Winter, zerstampft, gebrochen und befleckt zur Erde zurück. Andere wieder ruhen, unberührt und vereist, weiß und zitternd wie Schwäne auf dem Boden, aber von unten her zieht sie bereits das Erdreich hinab in die Tiefe. Sie krümmen sich, sie reißen sich los aus dem Schlamm, ein wenig weiter aber legen sie sich flach zu Boden, für immer. Das

trunk." [1] Not without a strong feeling of melancholy have I reread this passage from Jean-Paul Sartre.

It is completely dark. The black of the sky and the darkness of the unlit parts of the city weave a velvet cloth on which countless twinkling diamonds of light are bedded. Spread out before me, they sparkle bluish white and Neapolitan yellow. White and red dots move between them along strange trajectories, disappearing here, reappearing there. An irregular horizon flickers across my Copan panorama and through the mild smog of light that picks out the clouds the sky appears. Around Praça República below me peddlers are building a makeshift town.

1. Translator's note.
Jean-Paul Sartre:
Nausea, New Directions
Publishing Corporation,
New York, p. 10

alles lässt sich gut anfassen. Manchmal betaste ich diese Papierfetzen ganz einfach, in dem ich sie betrachte, manchmal zerreiße ich sie, um ihr lang hingezogenes Knistern zu hören, oder – wenn sie sehr feucht sind – zünde ich sie an, was einige Mühe verursacht; dann streiche ich meine Schmutz starrenden Hände an einer Mauer oder einem Baumstamm ab.« Nicht ohne Melancholie habe ich diesen Absatz von Jean-Paul Sartre wieder gelesen.

Es ist vollständig dunkel. Das Schwarz des Himmels und die Dunkelheit der unbeleuchteten Flecken der Stadt weben ein Tuch, auf dem unzählige glitzernde Lichtdiamanten liegen. Vor mir ausgebreitet funkeln sie bläulich-weiß und neapelgelb. Dazwischen bewegen sich weiße und rote Punkte auf geheimnisvollen Bahnen, verschwinden, tauchen wieder auf. Das flimmernde Lichtband meines Copan Panoramas zeichnet einen unregelmäßig verlaufenden Horizont und im milden Lichtsmog gegen die Wolken erscheint der Himmel. Um die Praça da República unter mir bauen fliegende Händler eine provisorische Stadt auf.

04 This morning a layer of dense fog lies over the fields of houses, or perhaps it is low-lying cloud that has rolled across the mountain range on the other side of the city and is now dispersing over the buildings. The sky plunges towards me, a light-grey expanse of nothing, an immense, immeasurable shape that turns the lookout before my desk into a slightly concave stripe, its barely perceptible movements slowly forming a contour out of its vague, soft nothingness. White haze, shapeless and fleeting, drifts in between. Almost transparent, it reveals the presence of the virtually vanished city in the distance. Suddenly, imperceptibly, the sluggish light emerging from the cloud takes a turn, changing the thin paleness along the edge of the cloud into a deep, warm grey. Slowly, very slowly, the movements of the sky increase, the light becomes stronger, divides and draws the carpet of cloud, spreads it out, lowers it into the city as far as the tips of its highest buildings and places the geometrical landscape beneath it under a weightless, enveloping load. During the minutes that follow, an Aeolian peristalsis transforms the mass of clouds according to some heaven-made plan and disperses their rethickening shapelessness across the stage before my eyes. The noise slowly rises from the depths, growing louder and louder until it reaches its familiar monotonous pitch. The day has begun.

04   Heute Morgen liegt dichter Nebel über den Häuserfeldern, vielleicht sind es auch tiefe Wolken, die sich über die niedrige Bergkette jenseits der Stadt schoben und sich nun über den Häusern auflösen. Der Himmel stülpt sich mir entgegen, lichtgraues Nichts, eine einzige maßlose Form, die den Sehschlitz vor meinem Schreibtisch in ein leicht gewölbtes Band formt und deren kaum merkliche Bewegung aus der diffusen Weichheit eine Kontur bildet. Dazwischen treibt weißer Dunst, vertriebener, formloser Rest. Fast durchsichtig gibt er in der Distanz die Ahnung der nahezu verschwundenen Stadt preis. Unbemerkbar wendet sich plötzlich das träge Licht, das aus der Wolke drängt, schafft mühelos die Inversion und kippt entlang der Wolkenkante die dünne Helligkeit in tiefdunkles warmes Grau. Die Bewegungen des Himmels nehmen zeitlupenhaft zu, das Licht gewinnt an Stärke, teilt und zieht den Wolkenteppich, breitet ihn aus, senkt ihn in die Stadt bis auf die Spitzen ihrer höchsten Gebäude und umfängt die unter ihr liegende geometrische Landschaft mit schwereloser Last. In den folgenden Minuten verändert eine himmlische Peristaltik die Wolkenmasse nach äolisch bestimmten Plänen und verteilt die sich wieder verdichtende Formlosigkeit über die Bühne vor meinen Augen. Langsam steigt der Lärm aus der Tiefe und schwillt an zu gewohnt monotoner Frequenz. Der Tag hat begonnen.

05 Good Friday. The day stands still, nothing moves. The streets are empty, the shops are closed, everyone has gone. Nobody who doesn't have to be here would stay, except me, the homeless, the beggars, the poor and the old, whom no one has taken with them to the seaside, to Santos, São Sebastião, the Ilha Belha or Utabatuba. Not a single bar or restaurant hopes to do any business today. Not until the evening will the devout remainder of the population gather in front of the cathedral on Praça da Se, where, at dusk, the procession through the old heart of the city will begin. The sky is low and misty, a deep grey lies over the valley, not a ray of sunlight comes through. The religious festival weighs oppressively on the city, overwhelms it, paralyses it.

I am unable to work. Neither the courage nor the strength to take the paper from the shelf, where it is neatly stacked in its different formats. The longer it waits there the more difficult the decision to take it and use it. The urge to formulate builds up until it bursts. Out of the wish for a visible result grows the loathing for the wish. A sadistic impulse negates the intention to act as a primitive, slavish urge and suppresses the sensuous pleasure in creating things. An infernal triumph of self-denial! The attack is always arbitrary, and the preventive, reflexive instrument, namely the brain, can only be outwitted if one forbids it the opportunity to cajole the emotions, to constantly interfere in the intuitive flow of vegetative moods and labyrinths.

Nothing happens. The window is open. Cool air, mingled with kitchen fumes, blows gently into the room.

05 Karfreitag. Der Tag steht still, nichts bewegt sich. Die Straßen sind leer, die Geschäfte geschlossen, alle haben sich verabschiedet. Niemand, der nicht hier sein muss, würde bleiben, außer mir, den Obdachlosen, Bettlern, den Armen und Alten, die niemand mitgenommen hat ans Meer, nach Santos, São Sebastião, der Ilha Bela oder Ubatuba. Keine Bar, kein Restaurant, das sich heute Geschäfte erhofft. Erst der Abend wird den gläubigen Rest der Bevölkerung auf der Praça da Sé vor der Kathedrale versammeln, von dem aus bei beginnender Dunkelheit die Prozession durch die Altstadt beginnt. Der Himmel zeigt sich niedrig verschleiert, tiefes Grau liegt über dem Hochtal, kein Sonnenstrahl dringt durch. Die lähmende Last des Feiertages erdrückt die Stadt.

Ich kann nicht arbeiten. Kein Mut und keine Kraft das Papier aus dem Regal zu nehmen, wo die Formate sauber gestapelt lagern. Je länger sie warten, desto schwerer wird die Entscheidung, die Blätter zu nehmen. Der Drang nach Formulierung verdichtet sich im Kopf und zerplatzt. Aus dem Wunsch nach einem sichtbaren Ergebnis wächst die Abscheu vor dem Wunsch. Ein sadistischer Trieb verweigert die Absicht zur Handlung als niedrige, sklavische Lust und unterdrückt das sinnliche Vergnügen an der Entstehung der Dinge. Teuflischer Triumph der Entsagung! Der Angriff bleibt willkürlich und die Überlistung des verhindernden reflexiven Instrumentariums, des Hirns, will nur gelingen, wenn man ihm verbietet, die Emotion zu beschwatzen, sich stetig einzumischen in den intuitiven Fluss der vegetativen Stimmungen und Labyrinthe.

Es geschieht nichts. Das Fenster ist offen. Kühle Luft

From Praça República rises the broken echo of hammer blows and this mixes with the deep start-up roar of the buses, today's only guardians of the traffic, in the Avenida Ipiranga. Stripped to the waist, I feel a breath of wind glide over my body. Standing between free fall and me are my desk and the concrete ledge, nothing else.

I am not sure of myself. I am unable to read the lines on the drawing in front of me, their motives are not clear. How does displeasure show itself? How does nausea affect the drawing, where does the movement lead? The lines weave their way without clarity and remain mute. I cannot decipher their weaving, who does? The needle of the seismograph deflects and strikes the head of the casualty on the 28th floor. The *basso continuo* of a helicopter underscores the high pitch of the violin from the computer; the drawing pushes itself into the foreground and affords no protection. What determines its lines and shapes?

The whole city stares at me. Every day, the dark eye sockets of the windows gawk into my cell, silently, expressionlessly. In the distance they curl into the horizon, creep into the mountain forests; turn their backs on me. Three drawings, unfinished, the fourth one beside me.

A jackdaw dives slowly into the depths. Soaring on hot currents, a hawk spirals upwards in large circles. The next helicopter crosses my gaze. The procession begins to gather before the cathedral on Praça da Sé. Against my will I begin to draw.

strömt mit fremdem Küchendunst mild ins Zimmer. Von der Praça da República steigt das gebrochene Echo von Hammerschlägen auf und vermischt sich mit dem tiefen Röhren der anfahrenden Omnibusse, die auf der Avenida Ipiranga als einzige Hüter des Verkehrs die Straßen kontrollieren. Ein Hauch weht über meinen nackten Oberkörper. Zwischen mir und dem freien Fall bleiben nur der Schreibtisch und die Brüstung der Lamellen.

Ich bin meiner nicht sicher, kann die Linien auf der Zeichnung vor mir nicht lesen, kenne ihre Motive nicht. Wie macht sich der Verdruss bemerkbar, wie befällt der Ekel die Zeichnung, wohin führt die Bewegung? Das Liniengeflecht ist unklar und stumm, ich kann es nicht entziffern, wer soll es erkennen? Der Seismograph schlägt aus und trifft den Kopf des Verwundeten im 28. Stock. Der basso continuo eines Hubschraubers unterstreicht die Höhe der Violine aus dem Computer, die Zeichnung drängt in den Vordergrund und gewährt keinen Schutz. Was bestimmt ihre Formen?

Die Stadt starrt mich an. Jeden Tag glotzen die dunklen Augenhöhlen der Fenster in meine Wabe, stumm und ausdruckslos. In der Ferne krümmen sie sich in den Horizont, kriechen in die Wälder der Berge, zeigen mir den Rücken. Drei Zeichnungen unfertig, eine vierte neben mir.

Langsam stürzt sich eine Dohle in die Tiefe, in der Thermik gleitet ein Habicht in weiten Bögen schraubend aufwärts, der nächste Hubschrauber kreuzt den Blick. Auf der Praça da Sé beginnt sich die Prozession vor der Kathedrale zu sammeln. Gegen meinen Willen habe ich begonnen zu zeichnen.

06 The city is drenched in bright summer light. The east wind drives and scatters cumulus clouds in front of it, while in the west a golden shimmer turns the watery blue of the sky into a light turquoise. The morning haze hangs in the quarters of the city and, with the help of the shadow play performed by the fleeting clouds, makes them stand out from one another with striking clarity. Countless satellite towns emerge from the morning brightness. The world below me is in a weekend mood, peace and quiet prevail, not a sign of aggression. Forgotten are the fanatical pacifists, who during yesterday's pathetic Good Friday procession stood on the top of an open double-decker bus and roared "violencia não, paz sim!" into their megaphones, as though they wanted to convince the wretched crowd of their mission by sheer force. Next to an agitated, grey-bearded, long and curly-haired pacifist, who was clearly making a pretence of youthful vitality, stood a middle-aged Franciscan monk without qualities reading Christ's Passion with unctuous pathos, while the crowd, or rather that handful of wretched and needy citizens for whom faith alone can sustain their hope of a more just life in Paradise, fervently clung to their candles, the unsteady flames of which they sought to protect as they invoked with one voice succor and courage for their daily suffering.

Copan is a philosophy. With thirty-two floors, and more than seventy apartments on each floor, the building is a veritable town in itself with 5,000 inhabitants. A closed community, a privilege of the 1950s, and the first dwelling machine in South America after Le

06 Helles Sommerlicht liegt über der Stadt. Der Ostwind treibt offene Cummulus Wolken in kleinen Gruppen vor sich her, und im Westen bricht sich das wässrige Blau durch einen goldenen Schimmer in lichtes Türkis. Der morgendliche Dunst hängt in den Stadtteilen, die sich im Schattenspiel der ziehenden Wolken auffallend voneinander trennen. Unzählige Trabantenstädte lösen sich aus der Helligkeit. Unter mir zeigt sich die Welt in Wochenendstimmung nahezu lautlos friedlich ohne erkennbare Aggression. Vergessen der Appell der fanatischen Pazifisten, die während der erbärmlichen Karfreitagsprozession auf einem offenen Doppeldeckerbus stehend »violência não, paz sim!« in die Megaphone brüllten, als wollten sie mit Gewalt die klägliche Menge von ihrer Mission überzeugen. Neben dem agitierten Pazifisten in vollem grauschwarzen Bart, langem lockigen Haar und falschem Elan stand ein mittelalter Franziskaner ohne Eigenschaften, der die Leiden Christi salbungsvoll pathetisch vom Blatt las und die Menge, eher das Häuflein der Elenden und Bedürftigen der Stadt, für die einzig der Glaube die Hoffnung auf ein gerechteres Leben im Paradies wach hält, umklammerte inbrünstig die Kerzen, deren unstetes, gefährdetes Licht sie zu schützen trachteten, während sie sich im gemeinsamen Gesang Linderung und Mut für ihre täglichen Qualen erflehten.

Copan ist eine Weltanschauung. Mit mehr als siebzig Apartments pro Etage auf 32 Stockwerken wird das Gebäude zu einer Kleinstadt mit 5.000 Einwohnern. Eine geschlossene Gesellschaft, Privileg der 50er Jahre und die erste Wohnmaschine Südamerikas nach Le Corbusiers Clarté und der Cité Universitaire, die von der Vision neuen urba-

Corbusier's Clarté and the Cité Universitaire, which was filled with a new vision of urban life. The extravagant sensuality of its undulating form and its majestic elegance and grandeur rubs off on the people who live here and fills all who work in it, its managers and its caretakers, with pride. Intelligently decentralized by Oscar Niemeyer into six blocks from A to F, each with its own separate access and concierge reception, the Copan Building is like a hotel or an 'urban country club' of the 1950s. The small reception hall of Block D, for example, is furnished like a living room with a chandelier in the style of the fifties, the arms of which form a bunch of flowers with polished brass stalks and glass petals. A copy of a *Boy Fishing on a Beach* in the style of a Brazilian Murillo hangs on the wall in a heavy wooden frame finished in imitation gold leaf. Every concierge in the Copan Building is a loyal servant and strict master of his respective domain. Standing behind mahogany woodwork and polished brass, dressed in white shirts and black trousers, dignified yet friendly, they gesture towards the lifts, the 32 pushbuttons of which are numbered in pairs, each pushbutton affording access to two floors via an ascending and a descending ramp. 27/28 marks my floor.

Every morning I stand in the casa do café Florestan in the Copan and order a café media with milk and a sandwich or one of the hot pasties stuffed with ham, cheese, palm tips, chicken or meat. I enjoy the Florestan, this old-fashioned cult café, famous for its strong, whole roasted coffee beans and also one of the famous landmarks of the São Paulo of the fifties. Be-

nen Lebens erfüllt waren. Die extravagante Sinnlichkeit seiner Wellenform sowie die majestätische Eleganz seiner selbstverständlichen Erhabenheit übertragen sich auf die Menschen, die hier leben und erfüllt jene mit Stolz, die in ihm arbeiten, um es zu bewachen und zu betreuen. In der dezentralen Erschließung von sechs Blöcken von A bis F, von Oscar Niemeyer intelligent verteilt, die ihre eigenen Zugänge mit Rezeption und Concierge verwalten, erscheint das Copan wie ein Hotel oder wie ein städtischer ›Country Club‹ der fünfziger Jahre mit südamerikanisch lässiger Geschmeidigkeit. Die kleine Rezeption des Block D zum Beispiel ist eingerichtet wie ein Wohnzimmer mit einem funkelnden Lüster und dazugehörigen Armleuchten der 50er Jahre, die wie ein Strauß Blumen ihre polierten Messinghalme über die Halterung beugen und gläserne Blüten tragen. Dazwischen hängt die Kopie *Angelnder Knabe am Strand* in der Manier eines brasilianischen Murillo in schwerem Holzrahmen mit falschem Gold. Jeder Concierge im Copan ist seinem Reich ein treuer Diener und strenger Hüter. Hinter Mahagoni und glänzendem Messing in weißem Hemd und schwarzer Hose gewähren sie in würdevoller Freundlichkeit den Zugang zu den Fahrstühlen, deren 32 Knöpfe der Stockwerke paarweise angeordnet sind, so dass jedes Stockwerk über eine aufsteigende und herabführende Rampe 2 Ebenen zugleich verbindet. 27/28 ist mein Bereich.

Jeden Morgen stehe ich in der Casa do Café Floresta im Copan, bestelle einen Café media mit Milch und ein Sandwich oder eine der warmen Teigtaschen, mit Schinken, Käse, Palmspitzen, Huhn oder Fleisch gefüllt. Ich genieße dieses

hind the counter young mulatto girls sing and hum to the music that comes from the built-in loudspeakers in the dark-brown wooden paneling. The dueño stands in the tiny cashier's box and takes the orders, while one of the girls quickly wipes the floor between two coffees. The ordered pasties are brought in blue-and-white-striped, yellow-and-blue-pansy-petal-patterned porcelain dishes. The dishes themselves are bedded in raffia baskets of the same size in order to protect them against the hard granite of the counter top.

Florestan is where people meet, where they stand before a once black-and-white wallpaper depicting a life-size, idyllic scene from colonial times, a coffee harvest towards the end of the 19th century, seen from the gracefully uninvolved viewpoint of the plantation owners. The wallpaper has meanwhile taken on the chocolate shade of the wooden paneling, shrouding the café in the atmosphere of an almost unreal, indeterminable past.

Very quickly, and without visibly moving her lips, the young mulatto girl, dressed in a black-and-white uniform, the live image against the backdrop of the colonial wallpaper, the sublime projection of an unchanged social hierarchy, speaks to me. I fall into those soft, slushy-mushy 'sh' sounds that flow into each other like custard and cream. The language gives no words away. The letters melt as they dance on the full, sensuous lips, everything runs together, gently, joyfully, smilingly. Not exactly terra firma for the Indo-Germanic mind.

altmodische Floresta, Kultcafé, berühmt für seine scharfe, volle Röstung der Kaffeebohnen und auch als Wahrzeichen des São Paulo der 50er Jahre bekannt. Hinter dem Tresen singen und summen die jungen Mulattinnen die Lieder, die aus den eingebauten Lautsprechern der dunkelbraun gebeizten Holzvertäfelung klingen. Der Dueño steht in dem kleinen Kassenhäuschen und nimmt die Bestellungen entgegen, während eines der Mädchen flink zwischen zwei Cafés den Boden wischt. Die bestellten Teigtaschen werden in blauweißgestreiften Porzellan-Schälchen gebracht, auf deren Grund gelb-blaue Stiefmütterchenblüten strahlen. Die Schalen selbst sind in Bastkörbe gleicher Größe gebettet, um sie vor der Härte der Granitplatte des Tresens zu schützen.

Man trifft sich im Floresta, steht vor der ehemals schwarz-weißen Tapete einer lebensgroßen bukolisch anmutenden Kolonialszene, dem idyllischen Bild einer Kaffeeernte Ende des 19. Jahrhunderts aus der elegant unbeteiligten Sicht der Großgrundbesitzer, das inzwischen den schokoladenfarbenen Ton der Holzvertäfelung angenommen hat und die Atmosphäre in eine fast unwirkliche, undefinierte Vergangenheit hüllt.

Schnell, ohne sichtbare Mundbewegung spricht die junge Mulattin zu mir, schwarz-weiß uniformiert, ein lebendiges Bild vor der kolonialen Tapete, sublime Projektion unveränderter sozialer Hierarchie. Ich falle in den Matsch der weichen ›sch‹ Laute, die ineinander laufen wie flüssiger Pudding. Die Sprache gibt keine Worte preis, die Buchstaben verschmelzen tanzend auf den sinnlich gewölbten Lippen, alles mündet sanft ineinander, freudig und lächelnd. Kein fester Boden für den indogermanischen Geist.

07 Lead-grey Sunday. Shapeless as far the eye can see. Cool and colorless. Embedded in the layer of dust on my *brise soleil* are small pieces of plaster that have fallen from the ledge above. A few mosaic tiles, having detached themselves in an enduring process of separation over many years, lie like monuments in the valley of the surface. Their matt sheen, covered with a layer of dust, like fluffy cellulose wadding, swallows the light. Who looks after the desert in front of my window? For years, now, the plaster has been flaking off the edge of the upper ledge where the tropical humidity soaks into the concrete. The dirt and the weather blemish the beauty and precision of the building's geometry. Time intervenes and works on the calculated surfaces of the building, taunts them into an organic reaction, exposes them to the drift of the clouds and the light of the sun, makes them swell, breaks their smoothness. Unnoticed, the slow decay ages before my eyes. The desert of 21,000 Arabian tiles grows with every glance. Everything bothers me, the smallest pieces of mortar, the broken edges where the tiles are missing, the terrains of dust that spread out like the enigmatic landscape of Man Ray's *Élevage de poussière*, or even a single tiny aluminum ring from a ring-pull can, a surreal relic of consumerism of enormous presence. These tiny objects grow to infinite dimensions in my imagination, command my gaze and pile up before me. Only the window between us makes them inaccessible, as inaccessible as the city down below, the city which is now disappearing in the fog, withdrawing itself, making itself very small, all of a sudden incon-

07 Bleigrauer Sonntag. Formlose Weite, kühle Farblosigkeit. Der Staub auf meiner ›brise soleil‹ trägt kleine Brocken von abgefallenem Putz des darüber liegenden Bandes. Einzelne Mosaiksteine, die sich in jahrelanger, zäher Trennung gelöst haben, ruhen monumental in dem Tal der Fläche, deren matter Glanz, von einer Staubschicht bedeckt, wie flaumiger Zellstoff das Licht schluckt. Wer sorgt sich um die Wüste vor meinem Fenster? Seit Jahren blättert der Putz am Rand des oberen Bandes, dort, wo die tropische Feuchtigkeit nach innen zieht. Der Schmutz und die Witterung brechen die präzise Schönheit der geometrischen Konstruktion. Die Zeit greift ein und arbeitet an den technisch berechneten Oberflächen, reizt sie zu organischer Reaktion, setzt sie dem Zug der Wolken und dem Licht der Sonne aus, lässt sie anschwellen, bricht ihre Glätte. Unbemerkt altert der langsame Verfall vor meinen Augen. Mit jedem Blick wächst die Wüste der 21.000 arabisch geschmückten Steine. Ihre kleinsten Mörtelbrocken, die ausgebrochenen Ränder fehlender Steine, die Staublandschaften, die sich wie die geheimnisvollen Pläne der *Élevage de poussière* von Man Ray ausbreiten oder ein einzelner kleiner Aluminiumhenkel ohne Dose, surreales Konsumrelikt von gigantischer Anwesenheit, bereiten mir Kopfschmerzen. Die winzigen Gegenstände wachsen in unendliche Dimensionen der Vorstellung, schieben sich in den Blick und türmen sich vor mir auf. Nur das Fenster zwischen uns macht sie unerreichbar wie die Stadt unter mir, die im Nebel verschwindet, sich zurückzieht und klein macht – plötzlich unscheinbar, monoton und bleich. Wie kann man die un-

spicuous, monotonous and pale. How can one possibly bear the irrevocable presence of this permanently chronicled, anonymous breeding ground?

More silent than ever. The city is dead. Easter Sunday. Not a movement, not a sound, nothing. Silence. Heavy, undefined form. Two small, adjoining clouds dissolve as they pass before my eyes.

Should I take the drawings from the shelf?

The sun hangs low in the west. The pale yellow light of the afternoon pokes through the clouds, throwing a fan of rays over the mountainous horizon, while in the east the city turns a deep violet and bluish grey rain clouds gather on the other side. Before me soft, cool air enters my room through the open window. The air is pure; the sky broadens. Its light blue, between the warm grey of the clouds, immerses the horizontal gleam of the closing day in a yellowish orange. Venetian rococo over the metropolis.

Praça da Liberdade in the East Asian quarter of the city is filling up with Japanese outdoor cookingstalls.

Suddenly the sun rips the clouds apart and hurls its light into the ravines between the houses. More and more helicopters fill the sky. Like mechanical wasps they flit agitatedly across my panorama as though they are searching for my lookout slot as a landing pad, while I keep perfectly still in my beehive, making neither sign nor sound.

Next to me is one of my unfinished drawings, and next to that, on a plate, half a piece of cake. Danish pastry filled with currants and topped with grated co-

aufhebbare Anwesenheit der Chronik dieser anonymen Züchtungen ertragen?

Es ist still wie nie, die Stadt ist tot. Ostersonntag. Keine Bewegung, nichts, kein Laut. Stille. Schwere, diffuse Form. Zwei kleine aneinander hängende Wolken schieben sich vor mir durch das Bild und lösen sich auf.

Soll ich die Zeichnungen aus dem Regal nehmen?

Die Sonne steht tief im Westen. Das fahle, gelbe Nachmittagslicht bahnt sich durch die Wolken und wirft einen Strahlenfächer über den bergigen Horizont. Im Osten kippt die Stadt in tiefes Violett, blaugrau sammeln sich die Regenwolken auf der anderen Seite. Vor mir, durch das offene Fenster dringt weiche, kühle Luft in das Zimmer. Die Luft ist rein, der Himmel weitet sich. Helles Blau zwischen den warmen, lichtgrauen Wolken, das den horizontalen Glanz des späten Tages in gelbliches Orange taucht. Venezianisches Rokoko über der Metropole.

Auf der Praça da Liberdade, im ostasiatischen Zentrum der Stadt, drängen sich die Stände mit japanischen Garküchen.

Plötzlich reißt die Sonne den Himmel auf und schleudert ihr Licht in die Schluchten der Häuser. Der Hubschrauberverkehr nimmt gewaltig zu. Aufgeregt kreuzen die mechanischen Wespen mein Panorama, so, als suchten sie meinen Sehschlitz als Landeplatz, während ich mich im Bienenstock ruhig verhalte und keine Zeichen gebe.

Neben mir liegt eine der unfertigen Zeichnungen, daneben, auf einem Teller die Hälfte einer Kokosschnecke. Rosinenschnecken mit Kokosraspeln, cremig und süß aus

conut, creamy and sweet, from the Itiriki Bakery on Praça da Liberdade. I ignore the drawing, which lies on my desk, pretending not to notice it in spite of its constant presence in the corner of my left eye. Writing keeps it out of my way, but I am constantly involved in it all the same – I am inside it, mind and body. I leave it alone and concentrate on the light over the city, sitting naked in my five-castor armchair. The cold air is dry and pleasant after the sultry heat of the daytime, its sticky humidity having slowly melted away as the cold water of the shower tautened and smoothed my skin.

The curtain of clouds falls in pale carmine on the stage of the sky. Drawing back, it takes the clouds with it to the west and opens up the space. Clear blue, as far as the mountains, is now the color of the semi-circular backdrop. Suddenly it is instant twilight south of the equator. It is getting cold. I get dressed. I've been drawing in my head the whole day.

der Itiriki Bakery an der Praça da Liberdade. Ich übergehe die Zeichnung, die neben mir liegt. Ich tue so, als sähe ich sie nicht, obwohl sie im linken Augenwinkel ständig Aufmerksamkeit fordert. Ich schreibe mich von ihr weg, obwohl ich ständig in ihr bin und in ihr denke. Ich berühre sie nicht, konzentriere mich auf das Licht über der Stadt. Nackt sitze ich auf dem fünfarmigen Rollstuhl, die kalte Luft ist trocken und angenehm nach der schwülen Hitze des Tages, dessen klebrige Feuchtigkeit langsam unter der Dusche aufweicht, wenn der kalte Strahl die Haut spannt und glättet.

Der Wolkenvorhang fällt in blassem Karminrot über die Himmelsbühne, zieht sich zurück, nimmt die Wolken mit in den Westen und öffnet den Himmel. Klares Blau bis in die Berge im Halbkreis des Bildhintergrundes. Plötzlich der Überfall der Dämmerung südlich des Äquators. Es wird kalt, ich ziehe mich an. Im Kopf habe ich den ganzen Tag gezeichnet.

08 Writing about drawing does not make a drawing. There is no bridge that leads from the word to the image. Nothing happens. The stammered mass of lines gets caught between memory and imagination; the image fails to emerge, slips beyond my grasp. The hand wanders, falters, loses its way, has no sense of motion, finds no access.

Both hands are motionless. The eyes drift over the sheet. The mind is a blank. All movements end up at the beginning, return incessantly, flee back to square one, refuse to venture into new terrain. What was once the repetition of lonely paths leads to rigid, lifeless ornament. The expression is pale, meaningless. Again and again a new sheet, same format, same loathing. The invisible noise of the city comes in through the closed window, unwanted and with the same existential naturalness as the air that I breathe. I breathe the noise, glance at the pushed-aside drawings on the desk. Two drawings are lying on the floor. How can I get through to them? Is there nothing to report and, if there were, what would this nothing look like? The eternal recurrence of the same. Appearance does not deceive. It remains forever true to itself. One must wait without waiting.

The city does not reveal itself. Am I expecting too much, too quickly? The desert has no centre, and the centers of the great metropolises of the 19th and early 20th centuries have become those desolate points on the map, which during the 1950s and 60s, proudly proclaimed the economic upswing in a new, pragmatic architecture instead of preserving their historic sites. To-

08 Das Schreiben über die Zeichnung ergibt keine Zeichnung. Keine Brücke führt von der Schrift in das Bild. Nichts regt sich. Das Gestammel der Linien verfängt sich zwischen Erinnerung und Vorstellung, das Bild entgleitet, dringt nicht durch. Die Hand irrt, stockt, kennt die Richtung nicht, fühlt keine Bewegung, findet keinen Zugang.

Beide Hände ruhen. Der Blick wandert über das Papier, der Kopf ist leer. Alle Bewegungen münden in den Beginn, führen unablässig zurück, fliehen zum Ausgangspunkt und wagen sich nicht in neues Terrain. Die einstige Wiederholung einsamer Wege gerät zu Ornamenten, die starr und leblos Halt suchen. Der Ausdruck ist blass und nichts sagend. Immer wieder ein neues Blatt, gleiches Format, gleicher Ekel. Der unsichtbare Lärm der Stadt dringt durch die geschlossenen Fenster in meine Wohnung, unerwünscht und mit existentieller Selbstverständlichkeit, wie die Luft, die ich atme. Ich atme den Lärm, sehe die beiseite geschobenen Zeichnungen auf dem Tisch. Zwei Zeichnungen liegen auf dem Boden. Wie finde ich zu ihnen? Gibt es nichts zu berichten und wenn ja, wie sähe dieses Nichts aus? Die ewige Wiederkehr des gleichen, der Schein trügt nicht, er bleibt sich treu. Man muss warten, ohne zu warten.

Die Stadt indessen gibt sich nicht zu erkennen. Will ich auch hier zu viel, zu schnell? Die Wüste hat kein Zentrum, und die Zentren der großen Metropolen des 19. und frühen 20. Jahrhunderts sind verödete geographische Mittelpunkte, die in den 50er und 60er Jahren den wirtschaftlichen Aufschwung vor der historischen Bewahrung stolz in neuer, pragmatischer Architektur proklamierten. Heu-

day, between Praça República and Praça da Sé, the city is inundated with endless streams of peddlers selling cheap kitsch, cigarette lighters, pencils, chewing gum, spectacles, watches, electronic trash and fruit. They share this former historic centre with the homeless and the beggars who populate the pavements, wrapped in plastic sacks and squatting on scraps of cardboard. A stench of urine, sweat and filth fills the air. A journey through time to the backward-looking standstill of a peaceful yet disconsolate siege. The bourgeoisie retreats and leaves the terrain to its own devices, allowing it to turn into an open camp. Was it pragmatic indifference or the powerless political approval of a temporary migratory watershed for the socially disadvantaged? Almost nothing remains of the city's colonial beginnings. The 16th and 17th centuries have almost been completely erased. The few baroque churches are a paradox – Franciscan interiors, wooden, light-blue-painted vaulted ceilings in the naves, hardly any ornamentation, plain altars, bare walls. And then there is the cool and austere neo-Gothic atmosphere of the cathedral and other religious buildings. Like toys surrounded by small, dirty squares, they seem strangely idyllic in the midst of the high-rise buildings. In truth, they are the pale relics of an unlived tradition. The city remains anonymous, a gigantic, pragmatic manifesto, a practice-oriented laboratory, a benevolent growth that develops and spreads like a refinery. A jungle, in the well-guarded clearings of which amply protected prosperity interrupts the thicket. Since Oscar Niemeyer's Copan Building of 1950, or Lina

te ist die Region zwischen Praça da República und Praça da Sé von den endlosen Reihen der fliegenden Händler eingenommen, die billigen Kitsch, Feuerzeuge, Bleistifte, Kaugummi, Brillen, Uhren, elektronischen Tand und Obst anbieten. Sie teilen sich das ehemalige historische Zentrum mit den Obdachlosen und Bettlern, die auf Pappen, in Plastiksäcke gehüllt, die Bürgersteige bevölkern. Es riecht nach Urin, Schweiß und Dreck. Eine Zeitreise in den rückwärtsgewandten Stillstand einer friedlich-trostlosen Belagerung. Das Bürgertum zieht sich zurück und überlässt das Gebiet sich selbst, das sich in ein offenes Lager verwandelt. Pragmatische Gleichgültigkeit oder ohnmächtige politische Billigung einer Migration-Besiedelung als temporäres Auffangbecken sozialschwacher Strukturen? Fast nichts ist geblieben von den kolonialen Anfängen. Das 16. und 17. Jahrhundert sind nahezu vollständig getilgt, die wenigen Barockkirchen sind ein Paradoxon, franziskanische Ausstattung, hellblau gestrichene Holzgewölbe im Mittelschiff, kaum Schmuck, einfache Altäre, kahle Wände. Dazu bestimmt die karge, kühle Neugotik die Atmosphäre der Kathedrale und anderer Sakralbauten, die wie Spielzeug, von kleinen, schmutzigen Plätzen umgeben, inmitten der Hochhäuser merkwürdig idyllisch erscheinen. In Wahrheit sind sie blasse Relikte einer nicht gelebten Tradition. Die Stadt bleibt anonym, ein gigantisches pragmatisches Manifest, ein Praxis orientiertes Labor, ein gutartiges Geschwür, das sich wie eine Raffinerie entwickelt und ausdehnt. Ein Dschungel, in dessen wohlbehüteten Lichtungen mehrfach gesicherter Wohlstand das Dickicht unterbricht. Seit Oskar Niemeyers Copan Gebäude

Bo Bardi's SESC Pompeia of 1977, there have been few
works of contemporary architecture worth mentioning,
with the exception of Paulo Mendes da Rocha's MUBE
of 1988, the Museo Brasileiro da Escultura on the
Avenida Europa, the bold linear minimalism of which is
a veritable symbol of a contemporary, living culture.
Alas, it is politically stifled and remains unused; humiliated at the weekends by the flea markets it has to
house. Nothing to appease the eye, to uplift the mind.
What does one Pantheon weigh against 100,000
mediocre utility buildings!

As a conciliatory gesture, the sun lays a narrow
stripe of light on the *brise soleil* in front of my window.
The sky turns towards me, gleams in pale cerulean
blue. What is to be done with the drawing I have begun?
I cannot touch it any more. But how can I intervene oth-
erwise?

von 1950 oder Lina Bo Bardis SESC Pompéia von 1977 gibt es wenig nennenswerte zeitgenössische Architektur mit Ausnahme von Paulo Mendes da Rochas MUBE, 1988, dem Museu Brasileiro da Escultura an der Avenida Europa. Sein kühner linearer Minimalismus taugt zum kulturellen Wahrzeichen einer zeitgenössisch lebendigen Kultur, jedoch innenpolitisch erstickt und ungenützt, wird es an Wochenenden durch die Behausung von Flohmärkten, gedemütigt. Nichts, was das Auge beruhigt, was den Geist beflügelt und erhaben stimmt. Was wiegt ein Pantheon gegenüber 100.000 mittelmäßigen Nutzbauten!

Versöhnlich legt sich ein schmales Sonnenband auf die ›brise soleil‹ vor meinem Fenster, der Himmel neigt sich zu mir, strahlt in leichtem Coelinblau. Was geschieht mit der angefangenen Zeichnung? Ich kann sie nicht mehr berühren. Wie sollte ich eingreifen, wenn nicht durch Manipulation?

09   Again I have begun to draw. First attempts. Consolation for fools. Proof of existence? Café Floresta brings me back into the world, the world that demands the simple yet important actions and dealings of life: getting dressed, waiting for the lift, descending in its cabin of light-brown Formica imitation wood with its uniform, artificial grain and its brass framework polished to a gleam. "Um café media con leite e um sandwich." Purely routine, and I demonstrate it nonchalantly. 5 Reais, 30 Centavos. And then off in the taxi, into the day.

Too much reality in the city, too much damaged nature on its outskirts, too many things, too many hands. Everywhere the physical presence of incessant movement, everywhere the constant presence of people. They lie in the streets, on benches, between parked cars, in the entrances to underground stations, exhausted, tired of living. They sit on the pavement, in front of shops, in the market places, in the parks, everywhere, waiting for the end of waiting, for the end of the day, for whatever will give them reason or cause to get up and go. But where can they go? They talk away the day standing outside the shops. They run between the waiting cars at the traffic lights and wait patiently for someone to buy some small unnecessary thing from them. They stand at the doors of snack bars and the countless tiny luncheonettes. Somebody asks for a cigarette.

The city shoves me through the streets. I glide past everything. The cars, too, push past one another, flow sluggishly through the city's main arteries: Consolação, Rebouças, Henrique Schaumann, Avenida Brasil, Avenida Ipiranga. Everywhere people seem to be busy,

09 Wieder habe ich begonnen zu zeichnen. Erste Versuche. Trost für Idioten. Zeugnis von Existenz? Das Café Floresta führt mich in die Welt zurück, die die einfachen und wichtigen Handlungen des Lebens erfordern: Anziehen, auf den Fahrstuhl warten und in dem hellbraunen Resopal-Holzimitat mit der gleichmäßig künstlichen Maserung von glänzend polierten Messingleisten umrahmt in die Tiefe schaukeln. »Um café media con leite e um sandwich.« Reine Routine, die ich gelassen demonstriere. 5 Reais, 30 Centavos. Danach ins Taxi, in den Tag.

Zuviel Realität in der Stadt, zuviel geschundene Natur am Rand, zu viele Gegenstände, zu viele Hände. Die physische Präsenz unaufhörlicher Bewegung, die stetige Anwesenheit von Menschen überall. Sie liegen auf den Straßen, auf den Bänken, zwischen den parkenden Autos, in den Metro Eingängen, sie sind erschöpft und müde vom Leben. Sie sitzen auf der Straße, vor den Geschäften, auf den Märkten, in den Parkanlagen. Überall sitzen sie und warten auf das Ende des Wartens, auf das Ende des Tages, auf ein Ereignis, das ihnen Gelegenheit und Anlass böte aufzustehen. Wohin sollten sie gehen? Sie sprechen in den Tag, stehen vor den Geschäften. Sie laufen zwischen den wartenden Autos vor den Ampeln und warten geduldig, dass man ihnen eine unnötige Kleinigkeit abkauft. Sie stehen vor den Eingängen der Garküchen und den zahllosen kleinen Luncheonettes. Jemand bittet um eine Zigarette.

Die Stadt schiebt mich durch die Straßen, ich gleite an allem vorbei, auch die Autos schieben sich aneinander vorbei, fließen träge durch die Hauptschlagadern Consolação, Rebouças, Henrique Schaumann, Avenida Brasil, Avenida

working on things that were meant to be replaced not more than once, giving them a dozen lives. Not a single thing that cannot be reused, not a single thing that cannot be fed back into the cycle of unlimited usability. They burden themselves with fruit, pull barrows and carts, rummage through cheap goods at bargain counters, guard the entrances of banks, shopping malls, supermarkets, underground stations. There is someone in readiness for everything, and every someone has a thousand stand-ins who won't ever get a chance. It is this omnipresent readiness, where waiting is a mark of life, at once a sign of willing endeavor and an expression of the eager expectancy of the impossible, this infinite availability of absolutely everyone, which totally confuses the senses. An unobtrusive surplus of passive muscles. Too much body, too much skin. Firm breasts in tiny elastic tops, voluptuous women, sinewy men. The senses get caught up in the factual present, get stuck on real things. Everything seems literary, direct, real, here, at this moment, before me, in me. No way out. No room for imagination. Everything imaginable is already there, ever present, making itself seen a thousand times over, unwanted, forcing itself upon me, into me.

The lights don't go out, and the noise surrounds me like the monotonous roar of breakers, the endless cycle of the natural forces of civilization: the memory of the place and the memory to which the place calls itself are the determinants of my present coordinates.

What is left for the drawing if every space is already occupied and surrounded? There's no escaping. Even the sky is filled with the city.

Ipiranga. Überall sind die Menschen scheinbar beschäftigt, legen Hand an Teile, die zum einmaligen Austausch vorgesehen sind, und geben ihnen mehrfache Leben. Kein Ding, das nicht nutzbar wäre, nichts ohne Wiederkehr in den Zyklus der uneingeschränkten Verwendbarkeit. Sie schleppen Früchte, ziehen Karren, vergraben sich in die Wühltische der Billigwaren, bewachen die Eingänge der Banken, die Shopping Zentren, den Supermarkt, die Metro Eingänge. Für alles steht Jemand bereit, und jeder Jemand hat tausend Ersatzmänner, die nie zum Einsatz kommen. Inmitten dieser allgegenwärtigen Bereitschaft, in der das Warten das Leben ausmacht als Zeichen willigen Bemühens und zugleich die gespannte Erwartung des Unmöglichen bedeutet, verwirrt die sich unendlich multiplizierende Verfügbarkeit aller die Sinne. Unaufdringlicher Überfluss passiver Muskeln. Zu viel Körper, zu viel Haut. Feste Brüste in kleinen elastischen Tops, üppige Frauen, sehnige Männer. Die Sinne verfangen sich in der Gegenwart der Tatsachen, kleben an den wirklichen Formen. Alles erscheint literarisch, direkt, wirklich, hier, in diesem Moment, vor mir, in mir. Kein Ausweg. Kein Raum für die Vorstellung. Alles stellt sich selbst vor, ist ständig anwesend, zeigt sich tausendfach ungewünscht, bedrängt mich und dringt in mich.

Die Lichter gehen nicht aus, der Lärm umgibt mich wie monoton tosende Brandung, stetiger Kreislauf der Naturgewalt der Zivilisation: Das Gedächtnis des Ortes und die Erinnerung, in die er sich ruft, mir als Zeichen der Bestimmung meiner gegenwärtigen Koordinaten.

Was bleibt der Zeichnung, wenn der Raum besetzt und umstellt ist? Kein Entrinnen, selbst der Himmel ist erfüllt von der Stadt.

10 Behind the window, the air is filled with the monotony of the traffic, which throbs in my temples. The powerful volume of sound amplifies to a uniform pitch. With my eyes closed, only the deep bass of the buses can be made out, a sonorous crescendo up to the first change of gear, ebbing slightly with the reduced revolutions of the higher gear and finally blending with sounds of higher pitch. The mass of undistinguishable sounds has now become compressed into a steady roar, pounding the ears like pressure at high altitude. The permanent throbbing close to the eardrums beats its way to the temples. I sit behind the window as if in a pressurized cabin.

The early haze of the new day robs the mountain ridge of its contour, dissolves it, decomposes it in the acid smog. The world vanishes in the immaculate blue of the rosy dawn.

The city is forming into line on the parade ground. The army of buildings stares expectantly towards the low-lying sun in the east. Each one towers in turn above the others, answering the morning roll call: "Present! – Present! – Present!" Present in their thousands upon thousands, lined up ready for the battle, unshakeable, impregnable, shoulder to shoulder, as straight as ramrods. The siege has begun. I withdraw behind the lookout of my bunker and wait to see what happens. The city's strategy is clear, the siege irrevocable. I am surrounded. Only the height of my position affords me protection. From here I can survey the field. Not a movement escapes me. Only the movements deep down below me are out of sight. I can only

10 Hinter dem Fensterglas ist die Luft erfüllt von der Monotonie des Verkehrs, der in den Schläfen pocht. Der mächtige Klangkörper schwillt an in eine gleichmäßige Tonlage, die bei geschlossenen Augen nur den tiefen Bass der Busse differenziert, ein sonores Crescendo bis zum Schaltvorgang, das dann bei abfallender Drehzahl des höheren Ganges leicht abebbt und in dem Klang der höheren Tonlagen aufgeht. Das undifferenzierbare Volumen aller Geräusche verdichtet sich jetzt zu einem gleichmäßigen Rauschen, das die Gehörgänge mit dem Überdruck großer Höhen belastet. Ständiges Pochen vor dem Trommelfell. Die Membrane ist in unruhige Schwingung versetzt, das Rauschen wandert in die Schläfen. Ich sitze hinter dem Fenster wie in einer Druckkammer.

Der frühe Dunst des Tages nimmt der Bergsilhouette die Kontur, löst sie auf, zersetzt sie im säurehaltigen Smog. Die Welt verschwindet im makellosen Blau der rosenblättrigen Morgenröte.

Die Stadt steht bei Fuß, scheint sich zu sammeln. Die Armee der Häuser blickt erwartungsvoll in die tiefe Sonne des Ostens. Einzeln ragen sie aus der Masse, jedes Gebäude für sich reagiert auf den Appell des Tages: »Hier, hier, hier.« Abertausendfache Präsenz, bereit für den Kampf, unverrückbar, uneinnehmbar dicht gestaffelt, Schulter an Schulter, kerzengerade. Die Belagerung hat begonnen. Ich ziehe mich zurück hinter den Sehschlitz meines Bunkers und beobachte abwartend. Die Strategie der Stadt ist eindeutig, die Belagerung unwiderrufbar. Ich bin umzingelt. Nur die Höhe meiner Position schützt mich, von hier aus überblicke ich das Feld, keine Bewegung entgeht mir.

hear them. No voices reach me. The city's weapon is the monotony of its soulless noises, striking my skull-cap like precisely dosed drops of water. Their regular dripping bursts the brain, trickles through the valleys of its convolutions, all the way to the back of my mind, filling, imperceptibly, the smallest cavities of the cranium. With the speed of a desert flood the noise wave spreads out, fills the wadies of the eye sockets, drenches the eyeballs, whirls around the convex inner surfaces of the vitreous bodies, vortexes back along the optic nerves. The torrent of noise heterodynes, finds no way out. Paralyzed, I am wholly under the spell of this siege from within. For over a hundred years this army has been waiting outside my window. The city knows no mercy. The heavens have no heart.

The first group of drawings is as good as finished. They have left me. They have been asserting the unknown, working against me. I am unable to understand their strangeness. Their restlessness. Their fleetingness. Their black humour, blacker than black. They defy the city and yet the city is all they talk about.

It looks as though the army is pulling back. Sure of itself, it has pitched camp in the light of the rising sun. The humid warmth of the coming day has put them in a conciliatory, ponderous mood. Unnoticed, I infiltrate their ranks. Resistance has begun.

The city laughs and beams. Along the narrow ribbon of the Consolação, which suddenly glints through a gap between some houses and then disappears just as suddenly in a left-hand bend, cars speed silently in

Unsichtbar bleiben allein die Bewegungen in der Tiefe, die ich nur hören kann. Keine Stimmen dringen zu mir. Die Waffe der Stadt besteht in der Monotonie ihrer seelenlosen Geräusche, die wie präzis dosiert fallende Wassertropfen meine Schädeldecke treffen. Der Gleichklang der fallenden Töne birst das Hirn, sickert durch die Täler der Hirnwindungen, dringt in den Hinterkopf und füllt unmerklich die kleinsten Hohlräume der Schädelkapsel. Mit der Geschwindigkeit einer Wüstenflut breitet sich die Geräuschwelle aus, füllt die Wadis der Augenhöhlen, prallt an die Augäpfel, verwirbelt an der inneren Wölbung der Glaskörper und wird entlang des Sehnervs zurückgeworfen. Der Tonschwall überlagert sich, findet keinen Weg nach draußen. Wie gelähmt verharre ich im Bann der inneren Umzingelung. Seit mehr als 100 Jahren wartet die Armee vor meinem Fenster. Die Stadt kennt keine Gnade, der Himmel hat kein Herz.

Die erste Gruppe der Zeichnungen ist nahezu abgeschlossen. Sie haben sich von mir getrennt, haben das Unbekannte durchgesetzt und gegen mich gearbeitet. Ich verstehe sie nicht in ihrer Fremdheit. Ihre Unruhe, die Flüchtigkeit, ihr schwarzer Humor, schwärzer als schwarz, wehren sich gegen die Stadt, und dennoch sprechen sie nur von ihr.

Es scheint, als zöge sich die Armee zurück. Selbstsicher lagert sie in der steigenden Sonne. Die feuchte Wärme des kommenden Tages stimmt sie versöhnlich, macht sie schwerfällig. Unbemerkt mische ich mich unter ihre Reihen. Der Widerstand beginnt.

Die Stadt lacht und strahlt. Auf dem schmalen Band

eight lanes in both directions. Immaculate blue hangs over the ocean and the millions of beach huts gleam in the light pastel shades of late summer. My penis stirs under my desk.

der Consolação, das in einer Häuserlücke aufblitzt und gleich wieder in einer Linkskurve im nächsten Häuserwall verschwindet, bewegen sich lautlos die Autos achtspurig in beide Richtungen. Makelloses Blau liegt über dem Meer, und die Millionen von Strandhäuschen leuchten in den hellen Pastellfarben des Spätsommers. Unter dem Schreibtisch regt sich mein Glied.

11 Continuity is the most effective torture. Permanence, in all its logical consistency, cruelly wears down resistance, not least because expectancy, the longing for interruption, sharpens the awareness of the helplessness that monotony brings and quickens those senses that perceive the slightest change as a sign of a possible interruption. Sensitivity, heightened by the awareness of one's own awareness, is the sister of torture; indeed, it is torture's clandestine accomplice. It is sensitivity that first permits a precise and subtle analysis of things perceived and brought into the focus of our attention. It is the attentive; organizing quality of perception that first recognizes permanent noise as the expression of an act or action, as the result of given conditions, as an arbitrarily unchangeable part of life and simultaneous subjection. Wildly raging in my apartment, surrounded yet unobserved by 18 million people, is the sheer madness of distant cacophonies. Even the noise made by the knife in my hand as it scrapes the last scrap of butter from the plastic tub jars like the screech of a chainsaw, splintering the hard, paper-thin plastic and increasing the volume to a hysterical crescendo. Like a siren, the gentle hum of the refrigerator transformer clashes with the noise of the breaking plastic, filling the kitchen cell with thunderous noise for seconds on end. And then, seemingly, peace and quiet. The pitch of these unexpected noises had interrupted the monotonous torture rising from the depths of the city, where only the staccato hooting of car horns was a match for the domestic strains from my kitchen. For a brief moment the continuum had

11 Kontinuität ist die effektivste Folter. Die Konsequenz des Dauerhaften ist von zermürbender Gewalt, wobei die Erwartung, die Sehnsucht nach Unterbrechung erst das Bewusstsein der Ausweglosigkeit der Monotonie schärft und jene Sinne alarmiert, die die geringste Veränderung als Zeichen einer möglichen Unterbrechung lesen. Die erhöhte Sensibilität, erregt durch das erkennende Sich-bewusst-werden, tritt als Schwester der Folter auf, sie ist ihre geheime Komplizin. Sie erst lässt zu, dass die aufmerksame Wahrnehmung die Dinge im grellen Schein der Fokussierung differenziert und in der Analyse bewertet. Erst die aufmerksame, ordnende Wahrnehmung erkennt den dauerhaften Ton als Ausdruck einer Handlung, als Resultat gegebener Bedingungen, willkürlich unveränderbarer Teil des Seins und des gleichzeitigen Ausgesetzt-Seins. In meinem Apartment, von 18 Millionen Menschen unbeobachtet umgeben, tobt der wilde Wahnsinn ferner Kakophonien. Selbst das Geräusch des Messers in meiner Hand, das über der Plastikkante der Schale den Rest der Butter abstreift, kreischt wie eine Motorsäge, die das papierdünne harte Plastik fasernd splittert und treibt die Phonkadenzen in hysterische Sphären. Sirenengleich mischt sich das weiche Summen des Kühlschrank-Transformators in das Geräusch des brechenden Plastiks, die Küchenzelle ist sekundenlang vom tosenden Lärm erfüllt. Dann Stille, scheinbare Beruhigung. Die unerwarteten Tonhöhen unterbrechen die monotone Folter, die aus dem Grund der Stadt dringt, und nur das kurze, kräftige Klangspektrum der Hupen erwidert die häuslichen Einsätze. Für einen Moment tritt das Kontinuum zurück,

beaten a retreat, leaving only the peaceful murmur of a basso continuo in the streets below.

The secret of outwitting torture is to vary the intensity of distraction. The sudden indifference towards the monotony of the pain makes it barely noticeable, almost extinguishes it. For the time being I feel safe. Only a brief moment of inattentiveness later – a wandering gaze across the noon haze – and the demon jumps out from behind my forehead and begins to conduct the orchestra with same effusive gestures as before. The heat makes my hands pour with sweat, it sticks between my fingers. A ribbon of black keeps forcing its way into my imagination. I think of the second group of drawings, a new format, renewed uncertainty, or an appetite for discovery?

I ignore the city. I refuse to have anything to do with it, devoting myself entirely to drawing. "To think that there are idiots who get consolation from the fine arts!"[2] Antoine Roquetin, himself the greatest of all such idiots, struggles against that inner voice on the light side of life that seeks consolation just in this way. It is the shame of despair, the defiant frenzy of uncertainty that makes him utter these words against himself and his inner conviction: outwardly superior, contemptuous of the world; inwardly inferior, humiliated. With his shame bravely swallowed, his inner doubts transform into the arrogant aloofness of conventional skepticism. And so many such shamed souls slink through the museums, spend their time in

2. Translator's note.
Ibid., p. 174

liegt wie ein friedlicher Generalbass auf den Straßen und murmelt.

Die Überlistung der Folter liegt in der variablen Intensität der Ablenkung. Die plötzlich eintretende Gleichgültigkeit gegenüber der monotonen Anstrengung der Belästigung macht diese fast ungeschehen, löscht sie aus. Ich wiege mich in Sicherheit. Eine kurze Unachtsamkeit später, der Blick in den Dunst des Mittags und der Dämon springt hinter der Stirn hervor, dirigiert das Orchester von neuem mit schwärmerisch ausladender Geste. Die Hitze treibt den Tau des Körpers in meine Hände und klebt zwischen den Fingern. Unentwegt drängt sich ein schwarzes Band in meine Vorstellung, ich denke an die zweite Gruppe der Zeichnungen, ein neues Format, neue Unsicherheit, oder die Lust auf Entdeckung?

Ich verweigere mich der Stadt. Ich ignoriere sie, widme mich der Zeichnung. »Wenn man sich vorstellt, dass es Narren gibt, die aus den schönen Künsten Trost schöpfen!« Antoine Roquetin, selbst der größte aller Narren, wehrt sich gegen seine innere Stimme, die auf der lichten Seite seiner Existenz gerade auf den Trost dieser Kunst wartet. Die Scham der Verzweiflung, der trotzige Taumel der Unsicherheit lässt ihn diesen Satz gegen sich und seine innere Überzeugung sprechen: souverän welt-verachtend nach außen, klein und gedemütigt nach innen. Die Scham tapfer geschluckt, so, wie viele mit ihm und der innere Zweifel verkehrt sich in hochmütige Distanz konventioneller Skepsis. Und so schleichen die beschämten Seelen durch die Museen, sitzen in den Konzertsälen und Theatern und referieren trost- und gnadenlos über den

the concert halls and theatres and cruelly air their
views on the status of the 'fine arts' so inaccessible to
them. As kindred spirits they embrace each other,
while nobody protects us from their repressed shame.

Status der ›schönen Künste‹, der sich ihnen verschließt. Einander umarmend suchen sie die verwandte Seele, und niemand schützt uns vor ihrer verdrängten Scham.

12   The early milky white haze blurs the gaze. The lookout seems more and more menacing. The feeling of being in a bunker gets stronger and stronger. The drawings are spread out before me, their expectations of me and my own expectations weigh me down. The mood vacillates between resistance and curiosity. The approaching weekend will make a change. I shall take time off, give myself a break, spend a few carefree days doing nothing. But this fleeting moment of yearning turns out to be one of absurd self-deception. The flâneur makes the rules, for leisure must be organized, taken according to a timetable. What then must be done with time? Can one write about one's work, account for it, put in words what is to be an image?

Down below buildings shoot out of the ground. Thirty-four degrees in the contrasting light of the afternoon. The hard shadows draw sharp contours into the dense maze. What a magnificent day. Then later the light softens. Gentle sweat spreads out over my body.

Back to the drawings. What is inscribing itself here, what urge is guiding my hand? Who deciphers the signs, who senses the emotion? What did Klee's *Pedagogical Sketchbook* or Delacroix's *Dictionnaire des Beaux-Arts* seek to do or be exactly? Circumscription? Definition? A reference map of the mind and the emotions. Are they the linguistic key to the image? The iconography of abstract signs and symbols is reduced to imprecise *gestalt* theories, and on this side of exile most aesthetic theories end in socio-political theses. Exile itself speaks only from the image. It describes the act of notation as an existential sign.

12 Milchig weich verwischt der frühe Dunst den Blick. Der Sehschlitz dräut, das Gefühl des Bunkers verdichtet sich. Die vor mir liegende Strecke der Zeichnungen, die Erwartung nach Erfüllung der Wünsche und die eigene Erwartung sind eine Bedrängung. Abwehr und Neugier wechseln ständig die Stimmung. Das Wochenende naht und wird Abwechslung bringen. Ich nehme mir frei, beurlaube mich, freue mich auf die freien, unbeschwerten Tage. Die flüchtige Sehnsucht entlarvt sich als absurder Selbstbetrug. Der Flaneur stellt die Regeln auf, die Muße will geordnet sein, der Stundenplan steht fest. Wohin mit der Zeit? Kann man über die Arbeit schreiben, Rechenschaft ablegen, formulieren, was Bild sein will?

Die Häuser schießen aus dem Boden. 34° im kontrastierenden Licht des Nachmittags. Die Schlagschatten zeichnen scharfe Konturen in das dichte Gewirr. Herrlicher Tag. Dann spätes, mildes Licht. Sanfter Schweiß breitet sich über den Körper.

Zurück zu den Zeichnungen. Welcher Text schreibt sich dort ein, welcher Drang führt die Hand? Wer entziffert die Zeichen, bannt die Emotion? Was genau wollte das *Pädagogische Skizzenbuch* Klees, das *Dictionaire des Beaux Arts* Delacriox'? Umkreisung? Einkreisung? Die Landkarte des Geistes und der Gefühle – eine Referenz. Sind das die Schlüssel der Sprache zum Bild? Die Ikonographie abstrakter Zeichen reduziert sich auf unpräzise Gestalttheorien, und die meisten ästhetischen Theorien enden in gesellschaftspolitischen Thesen diesseits des Exils. Das Exil selbst spricht erst aus dem Bild, es beschreibt den Akt der Notation als existentielles Zeichen.

What should I say? Back to drawing again. The Mikado
of nerves. I cannot do more, I cannot do less.

Was soll ich sagen? Wieder zurück in die Zeichnung. Das Mikado der Nerven. Mehr geht nicht, weniger geht nicht.

13 When does the thread break? When does life waive the essential solitude of observation? The social structure of the city leafs through pages as yet unopened: the transvestite quarter behind Praça República, Lina Bo Bardi's sculptural monolith near the Avenida Francisco Matarazzo, the leftist intellectual theatre TUCA in the Perdizes district, where the inspired intelligentsia meet, or the Sala São Paulo, a magnificent example of 19th century architecture not far from the restored railway station palace Estação da Luz and today the home of the city's symphony orchestra. Brahms and Tchaikovsky in the tropical metropolis, art's consolation in the highlands of Brazil.

The drawings are spread out before me like the blank pages of an unwritten book. The title page stares at me, patiently, without urgency. No constraint, just slight curiosity and reserve.

Whole days spent in taxis, buses and the underground. The distances are overwhelming. Stepping out of the house means losing a whole day. No early return after the prelude in the Floresta. A cool breath of morning breeze drifts through the room. Shall I stay, or shall I descend into the labyrinth? First to Santa Cecilia and then to Higienôpolis.

Taking action is a plunge into oblivion. Only the productivity of solitude can change the world. Rua Martinico Prado. Not taking action is a plunge into the realm of the imagination. Exile is the place of vision. "Get lost!" says a voice from the past. Preserve the unfamiliar between here and there. Thus, in their solitude, Curse and Grace are united at the same table. Who shall cast the dice?

13 Wann reißt der Faden? Wann verdrängt das Leben die wesentliche Einsamkeit der Beobachtung? Das soziale Netz blättert die ungesehenen Seiten der Stadt auf: das Viertel der Transvestiten hinter der Praça da República, die monolithische Bauskulptur von Lina Bo Bardi in der Nähe der Avenida Francisco Matarazzo, das linksintellektuelle Theater TUCA im Stadtteil Perdizes, wo sich die inspirierte Intelligenz der Stadt trifft, oder die Sala São Paulo in der Nähe des restaurierten Bahnhofspalastes Estação da Luz, Prunkstück des 19. Jahrhunderts, Heimat des Symphonieorchesters der Stadt. Brahms und Tschaikowsky in der tropischen Metropole, Trost der Kunst im Hochland Brasiliens.

Wie einzelne Seiten eines ungeschriebenen Buches liegen die Zeichnungen vor mir. Geduldig, ohne Hast blickt mich das Deckblatt an. Kein Zwang, leichte Neugier und Zurückhaltung.

Ganze Tage in den Taxis, den Bussen und in der Metro. Die Distanzen sind überwältigend, der Schritt aus dem Haus bedeutet den Verlust des Tages. Kein frühes Zurück nach dem Auftakt im Floresta. Der kühle Morgenwind streift durch das Zimmer. Bleibe ich, oder tauche ich ein in das Labyrinth – zuerst nach Santa Cecília und dann Higienópolis.

Die Handlung ist der Sturz ins Vergessen, nur die Produktivität der Einsamkeit verändert die Welt. Rua Martinico Prado. Das Nicht-Handeln führt in den Raum der Vorstellung, das Exil ist der Ort der Vision: »Verirren Sie sich!« klingt es aus der Vergangenheit. Die Fremde bewahren zwischen hier und dort. So sind Fluch und Gnade einsam am Tisch vereint. Wer wirft die Würfel?

The stack of drawings still lies there, untouched, 'airy nothing' to be turned into shapes by the poet's pen. The dream rises up from the depths, the sea of lights laps against the edge of nothing. Blackness over the city. My raised hide is at eye level with the horizon. Not a single voice. "Can you hear me?"

A tiny fly stumbles over the words, jumps between the letters, falls, makes another attempt at surmounting the sentences and dances across the page with nervous steps, dragging its shadow behind it. A dark fate in the dazzling light of the lamp.

Noch immer liegt der Stapel der Zeichnungen unberührt, ›airy nothing‹, das der Stift in eine Welt verwandelt. Aus der Tiefe steigt der Traum, das Lichtermeer schwappt an den Rand des Nichts. Schwärze über der Stadt. Mein Hochsitz trifft den Horizont auf Augenhöhe. Keine Stimme. »Hört ihr mich?«

Eine winzige Fliege stolpert über den Text, springt zwischen den Buchstaben, fällt, hebt von Neuem an die Sätze zu überwinden und tanzt in nervösem Schritt über die Seite, von ihrem Schatten verfolgt, ihn hinter sich her ziehend. Dunkles Schicksal im grellen Licht der Lampe.

14 Everything takes place at the edges, no center in sight. Then, later, the apprehension evaporates through the tip of the brush as it dances across the sheet.

Matinée at the Teatro Municipal. Thirty-eight legs and as many arms beneath the pre-Raphaelite rotunda, plus neo-Classical historicism with Baroque ornamentation and gilded rocaille. The organ with its Art Deco fascia, or a plain pattern from the fifties, solid brass in the floral latticework of the balconies. A hectic Modern Dance to Bach's Brandenburg Concert No. 4, then Mahler, Adagio of the 5th Symphony, and Benjamin Britten for desert.

Spent the afternoon socializing with friends in their garden. Too much conversation about the wind in one's hair.

14 Alles findet am Rand statt, keine Mitte in Sicht. Später löst sich die Beklemmung über den Tanz der Pinselspitze.

Matinée im Teatro Municipal. 38 Beine und eben so viele Arme unter dem präraffaelitischen Deckenrondo, dazu klassizistischer Historismus mit barockem Ornament und vergoldeten Rocaillen. Die Orgel mit Art-Deco-Verblendung oder einem schlichten Muster der 50er Jahre, schweres Messing im floralen Gitterwerk der Balkone. Erregter Modern Dance zu Bachs Brandenburgischem Konzert No. 4, dann Mahler, Adagio der 5. Symphonie und zum Nachtisch Benjamin Britten.

Den Nachmittag sozialer Parcours im Garten von Freunden. Zuviel Konversation über den Wind in den Haaren.

15 Under the asphalt of the city hordes of 'early birds' flock into the Orcus of the underground, gliding down the gentle slopes on moving staircases towards the colored signposts, red, green and blue, and then, as though magnetically poled, throng towards Jabaquara. The mass of heads falls into disciplined rows at the edge of the precipice, well over ten deep, obedient, stoically anonymous. It swells, like one huge, breathing body, growing dangerously large for the narrow space on which it stands. But then, from the dark depths, the head of a train emerges, drawing its long, sleek, scaly body noiselessly behind it until it comes to rest in the artificially lit, semi-circular tube of the station. It stands still for several seconds before opening its flank mechanically to the crowd. The ritual of the simultaneous, hundredfold conception is consummated as though of its own accord: the crowd unleashes its natural, pent-up energy, expanding into the countless openings of its patient host, its bodies now being jarred into motion, pressing, pushing, shoving forwards without restraint and at the same being sucked in by the gaping holes that divide and guide them like a funnel. In just a short, sudden, paroxysm the pressure is released, the mass individualized. In one wild determined forward charge it storms the flank, successful penetration now in sight. Only a short distance separates the countless heads from the momentarily essential fulfillment of their goal. Half surging forwards, half swept along by the others, they know that only a brief, calculated moment is given for the attack. Then the openings close. The victors, tightly packed and satis-

15   Unter dem Asphalt der Stadt bewegt sich die Menge mit ›Gold im Mund‹. Sie stürzt in den Orkus der Metro, gleitet die sanften Diagonalen der Abhänge auf bewegten Stufen hinab zu den farbigen Wegweisern Rot, Grün und Blau, und wie magnetisch gepolt zieht es die Herde nach Jabaquara. Diszipliniert sammelt sich das Feld der Köpfe am Rande des Abgrunds, schwemmt an in Reihen jenseits der Zehn, fügt sich in stoische Anonymität. Ein riesiger atmender Körper schwillt an, wächst und verdichtet sich bedrohlich auf dem schmalen Grat. Dann löst sich aus den Tiefen des Dunkels der Kopf eines Zuges. Wie ein Tier zieht er die schuppig gegliederte Länge seines glatten Körpers lautlos in das künstliche Licht des unterirdischen Halbrundes, kommt zur Ruhe, steht sekundenlang still. Dann öffnet er mechanisch seine Flanke und gibt sich der Menge preis. Das Ritual der hundertfach gleichzeitigen Empfängnis vollzieht sich automatisiert und mit gewalttätiger Natur entlädt sich der Drang der Menge. Stürmend dringt sie in die zahlreichen Öffnungen des geduldigen Wirtes. Die Körper geraten sturzartig in Bewegung, fließen, stoßen und schieben sich ungezügelt und werden gleichzeitig aufgesogen von dem Schlund der Öffnungen, die wie Trichter die Menge teilen und leiten. In einem kurzen, jähen Paroxysmus entlädt sich der Stau. Schlagartig individualisiert sich die Masse. In wildem, entschlossenem, Vorwärtsdrang stößt sie zu und drängt in die Flanke, das nahe Ziel des erfolgreichen Eindringens vor Augen. Eine kurze Distanz nur trennt die zahllosen Köpfe von der momentan existentiellen Erfüllung der Aufnahme. Halb vorwärts stürmend, halb mitgerissen, bleibt für

fied, slump into passive immobility, while the losers, left behind, renew their wait in lethargic silence. The train moves off, back into the darkness, taking its intruders to their unknown daily destinations along the line from Praça da Sé to Conceição.

Stopover in Rio. This is where the bird fills up for the equator.

Salvador de Bahia. Black Pearl. The salt of the seawater carries my body effortlessly – a metempsychosis between Africa and the New World. The treasures of tropical colonial architecture intoxicate the senses of today's conquistadores, and the unimagined blaze of colors fires the emotions. The city welcomes the stranger, enigmatically radiant, lethargically composed.

den gezielten Angriff eine kurze, berechnete Frist. Dann schließen sich die Öffnungen. Prall und befriedigt zwingt der erneute Stillstand die Sieger im Inneren zu wiederholter Passivität und lässt die zurückgebliebenen Verlierer in lethargisch stummem Verharren. Der Zug setzt sich in Bewegung. Zurück in das Dunkel entführt er die Eindringlinge zu den unbekannten Orten ihrer täglichen Bestimmung zwischen Praça da Sé und Conceição.

Zwischenstopp in Rio, hier füllt sich der Vogel in Richtung Äquator.

Salvador de Bahia. Schwarze Perle. Das Salz des Meeres trägt den Körper mühelos, Metempsychose zwischen Afrika und der Neuen Welt. Die tropischen Blüten der kolonialen Architektur berauschen die Sinne der neuzeitlichen Konquistadoren, und die Glut der ungeahnten Farbigkeit erhitzt das Gemüt. Rätselhaft strahlend und von träger Gelassenheit empfängt sie den Fremden.

16 Time for the senses. An early day in the sea, floating weightlessly in the rhythm of the long, barely perceptible swell. Energy, borne by the salt, converts into pure relaxation, every movement surfaces. The humid heat paralyses the brain's urge to think, lets the body sink into the sand. Traces of identity left behind, "traces qui humanisent le sol", as Dubuffet noted in his Sahara diary of 1948. The sea, the sky, the beach – a horizontal expanse. Beyond the rocks the city, black and colorful, agreeably garish and extrovert.

16 Zeit der Sinne. Früher Tag im Meer. Schwerelos wiegt es den Körper im Rhythmus der kaum wahrnehmbar langen Dünung. Getragen vom Salz, gleitet die Energie in vollendete Entspannung, jede Bewegung bleibt an der Oberfläche. Die feuchte Hitze lähmt den Drang des Hirns, drückt das Gewicht des Körpers in den Sand. Spuren zurückgelassener Identität, die den »Boden humanisieren«, wie Dubuffet 1948 in seinem Sahara Tagebuch notierte. Das Meer, der Himmel, der Strand – horizontale Weite. Jenseits der Felsen die Stadt, schwarz und farbig, wohltuend grell und extravertiert.

17 The provinces hold me up, stop me. Nothing happens. My clothes stick to my body in the heat, relaxing means overcoming obstacles, unessential solitude is sheer torture. The working utensils are in the drawer. The arsenal is cleared and tidy. My gaze registers the possibilities and leaves them unused.

17 Die Provinz hält mich auf, gebietet mir Einhalt. Nichts geschieht. Die Hitze klebt die Kleidung an den Körper, Entspannung gerät zur Überwindung, unwesentliche Einsamkeit ist eine Qual. In der Schublade liegen die Utensilien der Arbeit. Das Arsenal ist aufgeräumt, der Blick registriert die Möglichkeiten und lässt sie ungenutzt.

18 The provinces strike back with a remarkable stage play. The tourist is lured away by youth, beaming with strength and intelligence. Spellbound, the spectator involuntarily searches his memory, casts his mind back to himself, while the leaden ocean drags itself onto the shore.

Off to Praça da Sé and the Pelourinho, the Centro Historico, a UNESCO World Heritage Site. First wonderment, then inner emptiness. History, reduced to the backdrop that hides its reality, effaced, replaced by surrogate souvenirs – the global downsizing of real perspectives as an ironic shield against actual perception. What confronts the eye is the security zone of emblems, the anaesthetizing symbols of a globalized anti-culture that fill every available space. Piles upon piles of cheap and stupid merchandise, the products of monopolized, brainless mass production, flank the façades of the 17th and 18th centuries, block the entrances, turn wonderment, once aroused, into merciless consumption. Self-humiliation – that of the enslaved exploited vendors on the one hand, that of the half willingly enticed gawkers on the other – is expressed in their acceptance of their rôles, in the hopelessness of a situation from which no escape seems possible for either side.

The territory is staked out, the laws of commerce construed as living involvement, the participatory principle deemed honored once the condemned tourist carries away his trophy from this historical reservation. No communication other than the overwhelmingly vociferous praise of the goods offered. No historically

18 Mit bemerkenswertem Theater schlägt die Provinz zurück. Der Tourist wird von der Jugend entführt, kraftvoll und intelligent. Strahlend zieht sie den Zuschauer in den Bann der unfreiwilligen Erinnerungen zurück zu sich selbst. Unterdessen schleppt sich das Meer bleiern an den Strand.

Auf dem Weg zur Praça da Sé und zum Pelourinho, dem Centro Histórico, Weltkulturerbe der UNESCO. Nach dem Staunen die innere Leere. Geschichte, reduziert zur Kulisse, die sich vor die Wirklichkeit ihrer Erscheinung schiebt, unkennbar gemacht und ersetzt durch das Surrogat der Souvenirs – die globalisierte Verkleinerung wirklicher Perspektiven zum ironischen Schutz tatsächlicher Wahrnehmung. Vor das Auge drängt sich die Sicherheitszone der Embleme einer polyglott-uniformen Anti-Kultur, die alle verfügbaren Räume zur primären Betäubung besetzen. Billigwaren, monopolisierte Produktionsketten hirnloser Fließbandstupidität türmen und schichten sich vor die Fassaden des 17. und 18. Jahrhunderts, sperren den Zugang, lenken gewecktes Staunen in den erbarmungslosen Konsum. Die Erniedrigung der hörigen, entmündigten Anbieter und der halb freiwillig gezwungenen, geköderten Gaffer spricht aus den akzeptierten Rollen, liegt in der Ausweglosigkeit des Parcours, aus dem für den Statisten kein Entrinnen möglich scheint.

Das Territorium ist markiert, die Gesetze des Kommerz verstehen sich als Ausdruck gelebter Teilhaftigkeit: Das partizipatorische Prinzip wird erst in der Trophäe eingelöst, die der verurteilte Tourist aus den Reservaten der Geschichte entführt. Nur über die penetrante Anprei-

founded advertising. No pride in their historical identity. No words lost on history itself, on the period, the
style, the ingenious craftsmanship, the subtle choice
and aesthetic quality of the materials used for this colorful and beautiful architecture. Nothing said in praise
of the urban planning, the design of the arcades and
open spaces, the streets and the squares, proportion
and measure – the sublime symbols of secular and ec-
clesiastical hierarchies. The authenticity of history lies
buried beneath this soulless mimicry, these rubbish
piles of kitsch and bad taste. Nerve deadening and
sense depriving, these insults to true monuments become the ramparts of an inverted Cockaigne. The
yearning fools and dreamers, the last of the true travel-
ers, the consumers who attempt to eat this inedible,
globalized pap, will never set eyes on the realm of their
dreams, suffocated and poisoned by the stifling heap
of banality.

sung findet Kommunikation statt. Keine Werbung, kein Stolz spricht aus der Identität der Zeit. Keine Sprache für die Geschichte selbst, die Epoche, den Stil, das ingeniöse Handwerk, die subtile Wahl und die Ästhetik der Materialien der farbigen Schönheit der Baukunst. Kein Lob der urbanen Planung, für den Entwurf der Passagen und Freiräume, für die Straßen und Plätze, Proportion und Maß – sublime Symbole säkularer und ekklesiastischer Hierarchien. Die Authentizität der Geschichte liegt begraben unter der seelenlosen Mimikry, den Schuttbergen aus Kitsch und schlechtem Geschmack. Die Barrieren der Betäubung, der Sinnentleerung und die Beleidigung vor den wahren Monumenten wachsen zu Wällen eines verkehrten Schlaraffenlandes. Die sehnsüchtigen Toren und Fantasten, die letzten wahren Reisenden, die sich aufmachen, diese Wälle des zähen globalisierten Einheitsbreis zu schlucken, werden, durch den angehäuften Müll der Banalitäten vergiftet und erstickt, das Reich ihrer Träume nie erblicken.

19 Back amid the stones. The smog blurs the city. Later the field clears changing the way the horizon may be perceived – as the 'world' (Salvador) or as a 'detail' (São Paulo). The narrowness of the view across the sea of buildings immeasurably heightens the physical presence of things and, as it does so, inverts, broadens, becomes as free as the view across the bay of the Porto da Barra in Salvador, allowing the gaze to register the world as a detail.

Interrupted emotions.

Being away from the city had meant the loss of a temporary home. Even in exile, the process of setting up a place to live obeys an instinctive inner need and desire for security and stability. Here, too, actual recognition of the threat induces a state of relaxation, and this in turn asserts itself, struggles with the circumstances. Thinking erases memory, swaps it temporarily for the memoryless strategies of living in the present.

Like a tiny gnat on the ceiling a helicopter hangs in the distant sky, motionless between the clouds. A buzzard circles down into the depths and an airplane climbs eastwards out of the city.

From writing to drawing: the vague and confused murmur of the drawings, the eloquence of failure. Every beginning is an aimless journey across the expanse of the tiny format. The attempt at achieving the immense by focusing on what seems insignificant fails through dullness of thought and feeling. I take the one way out, out of my room, into the city. Left behind, on the floor, the sheets settle down to another long wait.

19 Zurück in den Steinen. Der Smog verwischt die Stadt, später lichtet sich das Feld für die Veränderung der Wahrnehmung des Horizontes als ›Welt‹ (Salvador) oder als ›Detail‹ (São Paulo). Die Enge des Blicks in das Meer der Gebäude steigert die physische Gegenwart der Dinge ins Unermessliche und kehrt sich um, so, wie der freie Blick über die Bucht des Porto da Barra in Salvador die Welt als Ausschnitt registriert.

Die Unterbrechung der Gefühle.

Der Weg aus der Stadt weist auf den Verlust der provisorischen Heimat. Selbst das sich Einrichten im Exil folgt einem instinktiven inneren Bedürfnis und Wunsch nach Sicherheit und Stabilität. Im tatsächlichen Erkennen der Bedrohung entsteht Entspannung auch hier, sie behauptet sich und ringt mit den Gegebenheiten. Das Denken löscht die Erinnerung, tauscht sie vorläufig gegen die gedächtnislosen Strategien gegenwärtigen Lebens.

Wie eine winzige Mücke an den Himmel geklebt, steht ein Hubschrauber in der Ferne bewegungslos zwischen den Wolken. Ein Bussard kreist sich in die Tiefe und gegen Osten steigt ein Flugzeug aus der Stadt.

Aus der Schrift in die Zeichnung: das diffuse Gemurmel der Zeichnungen, beredter Teil des Scheiterns. Jeder Anfang ist ein zielloser Weg über die Weite des kleinen Formates. Der Versuch des Immensen in der Fokussierung auf das scheinbar Unbedeutende misslingt durch die Unschärfe von Denken und Gefühl. Aus dem Zimmer führt der Weg in die Stadt. Weg von hier. Zurückgelassen liegen die Blätter auf dem Boden. Wieder das Warten.

20 The confusion shows no sign of letting up. I did not expect to see what I see, and what I see has no recognizable structure. Everything is fortuitous, disparate, dissonant. According to what expectations do we measure what we see, who judges, and by what criteria? Helplessly, amusingly, not to say cheerfully, things slide into a world of question marks.

It is this sudden loathing for the kiosk, the newspapers, the desperate slaves of society who marvel at the success of the parvenus and delight in the brutality of catastrophes. The feeling of loathing intensifies, directs itself with disquieting steadiness against the fulfillment of norms. The wanderer climbs a narrow ridge. Only at the top of the mountain is there room for him and his friends. His friends?

Suddenly, and very relaxedly, effortlessly, the way leads back into the drawing. The surface solidifies for the first time, and I can see the ground. Decisions are taken, patiently, layers of time become readable, shades take on subtle differences, the unpredictable inscribes itself. Rhythm, balance, tone. Night falls, the murmur of the city lingers.

20 Die Konfusion hält an. Ich erwarte nicht, was ich sehe, und was ich sehe hat keine erkennbare Struktur. Alles ist zufällig und von disparater Dissonanz. Nach welchen Erwartungen bemessen wir das Gesehene, wer urteilt darüber und nach welchen Kriterien? Ratlos und amüsant, geradezu vergnüglich entgleiten die Dinge in eine Welt der Fragezeichen.

Es ist dieser plötzliche Ekel vor dem Kiosk, vor den Zeitschriften, den verzweifelten Sklaven der Gesellschaft, die nur das etablierte Gelingen anbeten oder die köstliche Brutalität der Katastrophe verehren. Der Ekel verdichtet sich und keimt mit bedrohlicher Stetigkeit gegen die Erfüllung der Normen. Der Wanderer schreitet auf schmalem Grat, nur auf der Spitze des Berges ist Raum für ihn und seine Freunde. Seine Freunde?

Plötzlich führt der Weg entspannt und in völliger Ruhe in die Zeichnung. Die Oberfläche verdichtet sich zum ersten Mal, ich sehe den Grund. Geduldig treffen sich die Entscheidungen, Zeitschichten werden lesbar, Töne differenzieren sich, das Unvorhersehbare schreibt sich ein. Rhythmus, Zentrierung, Klang. Die Nacht fällt, das Gemurmel der Stadt hält an.

21 The lightening dawn, the intangible rest of the night, chattily stirs the day. Sleepless energy and uncontrolled delirium join forces with the senselessly early traffic of this Sunday morning. The city refuses to stand still and watch as the first rays of the sun flit over the curvature of the horizon to strike against its bulwarks.

A new beginning. A larger format. Another space. Three impulsive attempts. Surplus ballast that lies spread out before me. Clumsy exercises for compulsive motor functions. "Be inspired," says, unsuspectingly, the mobile phone in my hand: 8:19 a.m.

For hours the brightness of the day has been creeping into every corner, the Sunday is in full rage, only the clouds have kept their calm. Under the table my hand pushes my foreskin back over my glans, I feel the cool air on my body. Suddenly there is nothing else, only the air encircling me, dry and pleasant. The hand lies on the table, the fingers move, spread out, stretch out, stick to the tabletop. Dancing resiliently they exert pressure, flex their muscles. Suddenly they jump up, disappear from my field of vision, taking the hand with them.

Brighter and noisier still. Three drawings lie on the floor to the left and to the right, fantasies of demanding presence. Unexpectedly the demands are recognized and carried out.

The heat of the afternoon keeps the haze over the houses, the dry, penciled rays of light dissolve in the light blue between the towering clouds in the west, while in the east a diffused blaze of whitish grey ob-

21 Geschwätzig erhitzt, lichtet sich die Dämmerung. Der unbegreifbare Rest der Nacht, schlaflose Energie und ungesteuertes Delirium versammeln sich lautstark und mischen sich in den sinnlos frühen Verkehr des Sonntagmorgens. Das Zentrum verweigert den Stillstand, während die ersten Strahlen der Sonne über die Krümmung des Horizontes fliegen und gegen das Bollwerk der Stadt prallen.

Neuer Beginn. Größeres Format, ein anderer Raum. Drei impulsive Versuche, überschüssiger Ballast, der sich vor mir ausbreitet. Ungelenke Übungen zwanghafter Motorik. »Be inspired« sagt das Handy ahnungslos in meiner Hand: 8:19 Uhr.

Seit Stunden kriecht die Helligkeit in alle Winkel, der Sonntag brüllt, nur die Wolken bewahren die Ruhe. Unter dem Tisch schiebt meine Hand die Vorhaut über der Eichel zurück, die kühle Luft berührt den Oberkörper. Plötzlich gar nichts, außer der Luft, die den Körper umkreist, trocken und angenehm. Die Hand liegt auf dem Tisch. Die Finger breiten sich aus, bewegen sich, gestreckt kleben sie an der Fläche des Tisches. Elastisch tanzend üben sie Druck aus und spielen mit den Muskeln. Plötzlich springen sie auf, verabschieden sich und nehmen die Hand aus dem Blickfeld.

Noch mehr Helligkeit, noch mehr Lärm. Drei Zeichnungen liegen auf dem Boden, links und rechts, Hirngespinste mit fordernder Anwesenheit. Unvermutet erkennt man die Forderung und führt sie aus.

Die Hitze des Nachmittags hält den Dunst über den Häusern, das trockene Licht bündelt die Strahlen, löst sich

structs the view. Hard to breathe, everything is still, the air hardly stirs. Energy drains, movements slow down, the room stares at me, the objects gawk stupidly, everything is magnified. The brain jerks, obeys the signals.

in das helle Blau zwischen den hoch stehenden Wolken-
türmen im Westen, und im Osten verdeckt das gleißend
diffuse Weißgrau die Sicht. Schwerer Atem, alles steht
still, kaum regt sich die Luft. Die Bewegungen verlangsa-
men sich kraftlos, das Zimmer starrt mich an, die Gegenstände glotzen blöde, alles vergrößert sich. Ruckartig
folgt das Gehirn den Signalen.

22 A glorious day. The factory is running at full speed. All the machines are roaring away. The lookout is part of life and the unreality of the location, my desk suspended on the 28th floor, measuring 79 x 160 cm, is the territory, the temporary landing strip for reality and fantasy.

Keen observation concentrates the sensitivity of perception like a whirlpool, gets to the skin of things, overcomes the natural distance and eliminates the protection interspaces afford. In the alarmed state of seeing without filters, even the smallest detail assumes Pantagruelian significance and fractal perception enlarges every partial view to dimensions of infinity hitherto unknown. In this step-by-step repetition of repetition the world becomes visible with polymorphous sharpness and skins the things mercilessly: the inflamed optic nerve wanders aimlessly with absolute concentration. A square centimeter of mosaic, the window of a distant building, the silhouette of a wooded mountain ridge detach themselves involuntarily from their syncretistic field to become landscapes in their own right, self-willed, compressed by the intensity of perception into crystalline microcosms of blackness, space and materiality. The unbearable diversity of microscopic nature rages in the valleys of the quarks. The maelstrom of this absolute, unconditioned way of seeing draws the gaze into the darkness of the new, into the never-seen-before, into the light of the shadows. Unawares and with uncommon rapidity of approach, the eye is drawn in more and more deeply, towards the tactile structures of the invisible, where, in free fall, it

22 Strahlender Tag. Die Fabrik läuft auf Hochtouren, alle Maschinen dröhnen. Der Sehschlitz ist Teil des Lebens und die Unwirklichkeit des Standortes, mein im 28. Stock suspendierter Schreibtisch, 79 x 160 cm, bemisst das Territorium: vorläufiger Landeplatz von Wirklichkeit und Phantasie.

Wie ein Strudel bündelt die aufmerksame Beobachtung die Empfindlichkeit der Wahrnehmung, zieht sie an die Haut der Dinge, bricht die natürliche Distanz und hebt den Schutz der Zwischenräume auf. Im alarmierten Zustand filterlosen Sehens gewinnt das kleinste Detail pantagruelsche Bedeutung, und die fraktale Wahrnehmung vergrößert jeden Ausschnitt in nie gekannte Dimensionen der Unendlichkeit. Die Welt trennt sich in der schrittweisen Wiederholung der Wiederholung in polymorpher Schärfe und häutet die Dinge schonungslos: Der entzündete Sehnerv irrt konzentriert und ohne Ziel. Ein Quadratzentimeter Mosaik, das Fenster eines entfernten Hauses, die Silhouette eines bewaldeten Bergrückens lösen sich unfreiwillig aus dem synkretistischen Feld und werden zu eigensinnigen Landschaften unendlicher Schattierungen, die sich in der Tiefe der Wahrnehmung zu kristallinen Mikrokosmen von Schwärze, Raum und Stofflichkeit komprimieren. In den Tälern der Quarks wütet die unerträgliche Vielfalt mikroskopischer Natur. Der Malstrom dieses unbedingten Sehens reißt den Blick mit sich fort, zieht ihn in das Dunkel des Neuen, des nie Gesehenen und eröffnet das Licht der Schatten. Tiefer und immer tiefer, ohne Ahnung und mit rasanter Annäherung führt er an die taktilen Strukturen unsichtbarer Gefilde,

registers with feverish sensitivity the changes in blacker than black nuances of shade. Cautiously, and at the moment of its highest velocity, this free fall reverses, whirls upwards, defying the laws of gravity, robbing one of one's senses in the very core of the extreme and enforcing utmost tranquility in no man's land. Only the constancy of the directed gaze can save the dancer, shipwrecked in the centrifugal current of the maelstrom.

wo das Auge in fiebriger Sensibilität schwärzer als Schwarz den Wechsel nicht wahrnehmbarer Schattierungen im freien Fall registriert. Abwartend verkehrt sich in der äußersten Geschwindigkeit der Bewegung der Fall in rasantem Taumel in den Aufwind einer Steigung. Der Strudel dehnt die Gesetze der Gravität, raubt die Sinne im Auge der Extreme und zwingt zu äußerster Ruhe im Niemandsland. Nur die Konstante des gerichteten Blicks rettet den Tänzer, Schiffbrüchiger in den Fliehkräften des Wirbels.

23 In the heat and the noise the eye strays to and fro between the left and right, defining verticals of the cell. The futility of the daily re-beginning speaks through the absurd existence of the drawings, which cover the floor with their own worlds. Like strange desert islands they lie around the room, which in the sparseness of its pragmatic setting seems totally unprepared for the dense gravitational fields of emotion that are strewn across the floor. No consolation is desired, no reception possible.

What is keeping me here? And is 'here' the crucial word, or is it the action which is calling itself into question, generally, quite regardless of the choice of place? Within these 34 square meters of reservation, the discovery of the world repeats itself again and again, the 'taste of a Madeleine' invades the senses, the ego is explored against its will for the umpteenth time, and introspection joins forces with the perception of images set free by self-searching, hallucinatory consciousness. A world of 'pure sensation' spreads across the drawings. Later it will be scrutinized by the viewer and reduced to those archaic forms that filter through the drawing's complex, multilayered weave and exist in his projection alone. Thus the viewer's image suppresses the artist's image, and in so doing obscures or erases the primal energies and forfeits the inner timbre of precisely the image that he is in fact seeking.

23 In der Hitze und dem Lärm schweift der Blick absichtslos von der linken Begrenzung der Wabe zur rechten und wieder zurück. Die Vergeblichkeit des täglichen Wiederbeginns spricht aus der Absurdität der Existenz der Zeichnungen, die den Fußboden mit ihrer Welt bedecken Wie fremde, einsame Inseln liegen sie in dem Zimmer, das in der sparsamen Wahl seiner pragmatischen Einrichtung unvorbereitet erscheint für die auf dem Boden verstreuten dichten Gravitationsfelder der Emotion. Kein Trost ist erwünscht, keine Aufnahme möglich.

Was hält mich hier? Und ist das ›Hier‹ entscheidend für die Frage, oder ist es die Handlung, die sich frei von der Wahl des Ortes generell in Frage stellt? Im Reservat der 34 qm wiederholt sich die Entdeckung der Welt, der ›Duft einer Madeleine‹ umfängt die Sinne, es ist die unfreiwillige Entdeckung des ICH zum x-ten Mal, und mit der prüfenden Introspektion verbindet sich die Wahrnehmung jener Bilder, die das forschend halluzinierende Bewusstsein entlässt. Das Reich der ›reinen Empfindung‹ breitet sich aus in der Zeichnung. Später wird es durch den Betrachter sorgfältig auf jene archaischen Gestaltformen überprüft und reduziert, die er aus dem vielschichtig gewobenem Netz des Bildes destilliert und die allein in seiner Projektion existieren. So schiebt sich das Bild des Betrachters vor das Bild des Künstlers, eine Überblendung entsteht, ein zweites Bild, in dem der Betrachter jene ursprünglichen Energien verschleiert oder löscht und so den inneren Klang des Bildes verliert, nach dem er in Wirklichkeit sucht.

24 The incessantly raging traffic cascades into the city below me with ear-splitting violence, its noise dulling the senses, as though covering them with a thick coating.

Situated in the southeast, on the other side of the Rio Pinheiros, which together with the Rio Tietê was once the city's boundary, is the residential district of Morumbí. Its gently rolling hills gradually gain height as they meet the mountain forests that today mark the city's boundary. The huge bamboo groves, the spreading rubber trees and the sumamé trees with their thick belts of air roots immerse Lina Bo Bardi's 'Glass House' in the tranquility of a botanical garden. Built by the architect in Bauhaus style in 1950, her residence stands on iron stilts above a steep incline. The rich natural vegetation, the organic density of the fleshy leaves, the impenetrable walls of fresh bamboo and the soft layers of humus that yield underfoot exude a calm, imperturbable force.

The eye glides over the mosaic tiles of my *brise soleil* and takes off, air-borne, across the endless expanse of towering stones. Not a blade of grass far and wide, not a branch or twig, not a leaf, no organic discoloration, no natural curves, nothing stirs, no seed finds its way into the joints. The expanse of towers swallows up the horizon a million times over and the low sky of the morning arches over the desert.

Somewhere in the Copan Building a hammer strikes a chisel, its high-pitched, metallic rhythm clearly audible above the electric hum of the traffic, while a second cadence of blows, slightly staggered, responds with a

24 Der unaufhörlich tosende Wasserfall des Verkehrs bricht mit betäubender Gewalt unter mir in die Stadt. Im Auge der Geräusche schwirrt das Trommelfell, und wie ein Belag bedeckt der Lärmschwall die Sinne, pelzig und dumpf.

Jenseits des Rio Pinheiros, der mit dem Rio Tietê einst die Stadt begrenzte, liegt im Südosten das Villenviertel Morumbi mit seinen sanften Hügeln, die sich allmählich anwachsend bis in die Bergwälder der heutigen Stadtgrenze erstrecken. Die Stille der riesigen Bambusstauden, der ausladenden Gummibäume und der Sumamé Bäume mit ihrem dichten Gürtel von Luftwurzeln umfängt das Glashaus von Lina Bo Bardi wie ein botanischer Garten. 1950 entwarf die Architektin ihr Wohnhaus im Bauhausstil, ein Pfahlhaus auf eisernen Röhren über den steilen Hang gestellt. Die vegetative Fülle der Natur, die organische Dichte der fleischigen Blätter, die undurchdringbaren Wände des frischen Bambus und der weiche, nachgebende Tritt auf den Humusschichten des waldigen Bodens atmen eine stille unbeirrbare Kraft.

Der Blick gleitet über die Mosaiksteine meiner Sonnenblende und fliegt ohne Bodenhaftung in die endlose Weite der aufgetürmten Steine. Kein Halm weit und breit, kein Zweig, kein Blatt, keine organische Färbung, keine natürliche Krümmung, nichts regt sich, kein Samen dringt zwischen die Fugen. Die Weite der Türme schluckt den Horizont millionenfach und über der Wüste wölbt sich der tiefe Himmel des Morgens.

Irgendwo im Copan trifft ein Hammer den Meißel. Hell liegt der metallische Rhythmus der Schläge über dem

muffled, hollow sound. No sign of fatigue. The lamenting drone of a siren intervenes, then an alarm spirals briefly into the ether. Only the helicopters silhouetted against the milky shadows of the mountain ridges move soundlessly in the distance.

In vain the rhythm of the hand defends itself in the cacophonic expanse of infinite space. Dissonance, dark and gloomy, abrupt and harsh, intrudes into the drawing, rendering the gaze helpless as it observes what is happening. Nobody intervenes, only the hand reacts. The line moves unwaveringly across the surface, clarity gains in contour, guides the pencil, leads it against the weight of the world.

Strom der Motoren, und in versetztem Intervall fällt eine zweite Schlagkadenz auf einen dumpfen Hohlraum. Keine Ermüdung ist spürbar. Eine Sirene mischt sich ein, leiernd und jammervoll, dann windet sich eine kurze Alarmspirale in den Äther. Nur die Hubschrauber vor dem milchigen Schatten der Bergrücken bewegen sich tonlos schemenhaft in der Distanz.

Vergeblich wehrt sich der Rhythmus der Hand in der kakophonischen Weite des endlichen Raumes. Schwarz und düster, abrupt und hart gräbt sich die Dissonanz in die Zeichnung, ohnmächtig versichert sich der Blick des Geschehens. Niemand greift ein, nur die Hand hält dagegen. Unbeirrbar zieht die Linie über die Fläche, die Klarheit gewinnt an Kontur, führt den Stift gegen die Wucht der Welt.

25 Nothing special. Repetition of the same. Not a cloud in the sky. Over 30 degrees every day.

Greater density in the last group of drawings, yet not one color asserts itself. Black Nanjing ink, pencil, white watercolor. The severity of the city makes its imprint, smudges the color; the mass swallows the individual, nothing comes to the fore. Even Iberapuera Park is dominated by the pale dirty white of Oscar Niemeyer's architecture. The sun bleaches every brilliance, drains the colors of their energy, washes them pure, like the moon in the Songs of Gurre. Shimmering pale and matt, discreetly camouflaged against the energy of the light, the architecture defies the tropical climate. Thus, grey and unadorned, present only through its mass, the artefact withstands the forces of nature. The city ducks down low, turns its back against the light, not retreating from it but rather herding together in countless, indescribably expansive numbers in the high-lying valley between the Tietê, Paraná and Yguatemy rivers, which it then degrades to poisoned, stinking rivulets. Even at its edges the stony fabric does not fray. After hours no ground is gained, the center and the outskirts are identical, a thousand-in-one villages, a thousand-in-one cities – the fatal history of a century, an absurd living world. City state, pragmatism, Darwinism. From the bus into the helicopter.

Nothing survives. No space to be oneself. History is erased, sacrificed, stifled, murdered in the abysses. Even the parks are small towns, crisscrossed with broad strips of asphalt for the onslaught of regenerating joggers, skaters, cyclists that glide past one an-

25 Nichts Besonderes. Die Wiederholung des Gleichen. Keine Wolke am Himmel. Jeder Tag jenseits der 30°.

Die letzte Gruppe der Zeichnungen verdichtet sich, aber keine Farbe setzt sich durch. Schwarze Nanking Tusche, Bleistift und weißes Aquarell. Die Härte der Stadt prägt sich ein, verwischt die Farben, die Masse schluckt das Individuum, nichts tritt hervor. Auch im Iberapuera Park dominiert das fahle schmutzige Weiß der Architektur Oscar Niemeyers. Die Sonne bleicht jede Brillanz, entzieht den Farben die Kraft, wäscht sie rein, wie der Mond die Gurrelieder. In blassem, mattem Glanz trotzt die Architektur dem tropischen Klima, tarnt sich unauffällig vor der Energie des Lichts. Grau und schmucklos, nur durch Masse präsent besteht der künstliche Entwurf die Gewalt der Natur. Die Stadt duckt sich, richtet ihren Rücken gegen das Licht, aber weicht nicht vor ihm, sie rottet sich zusammen, zahllos und von unbeschreibbarer Ausdehnung bettet sie sich in das Hochtal zwischen die Flüsse Tietê, Paraná und Iguatemy, die sie zu vergifteten, stinkenden Rinnsalen degradiert. Auch zum Rand dünnt sich das steinerne Gewebe nicht aus. Nach Stunden ist kein Boden gewonnen, Zentrum und Ausdehnung sind identisch, tausend Dörfer, tausend Städte in dieser einen – die fatale Geschichte eines Jahrhunderts, eine absurde, lebendige Welt. Stadtstaat, Pragmatismus, Darwinismus. Vom Bus in den Hubschrauber.

Nichts besteht. Kein Freiraum in Sicht. Geschichte wird getilgt, geopfert und in den Schluchten erstickt. Selbst die Parks sind kleine Städte, durchzogen von breiten Asphaltbändern für den Ansturm der regenerieren-

other in the coolness of the night, shadows taking their bodies for a run or a ride. Distance. Only the observer keeps his distance, does not lose himself in the crowd, resists the turmoil, or else he gives up and drowns with all the others in crushed limes and cachaza. Gone. On his way to delirium.

Awareness of repetition does not point to the repetition itself but rather to the ascertainment of its discovery as a phenomenon. As an exercise, as a means of perceiving more strongly, repetition forfeits the impulse of the initial act and at the same time gains, through the realization of the impulse, intensity – and this in turn results in a conscious deceleration of the situation. The difference arises at the moment of the decided return and succeeds only in the openness of its approval, not in its anticipated execution. Thus a return presents itself as a possibility and not as an affirmation.

The three drawings on the floor are a meaningful warning: have been going too close to things. Between the passion of the emotions and the dispassion of the intellect, the mind either lets itself be guided by itself or gives preference to the body. The dichotomy seems to lie in the accursed incompatibility of forces. Who decides on failure or success, or on failure as success?

den Jogger, Skater, Fahrradfahrer, die in der Kühle der Nacht schemenhaft aneinander vorbei gleiten und ihre Körper spazieren führen. Distanz. Nur der Beobachter verliert sich nicht in der Menge, widersteht dem Schwindel, oder er gibt auf und ertränkt sich mit all den anderen in den mit Cachaza getränkten Limonen. Weg, ab ins Delirium.

Das Bewusstsein der Wiederholung weist nicht auf die Wiederholung, sondern auf die Vergewisserung der Entdeckung als Manifestation. Als Einübung, als bekräftigende Wahrnehmung verliert die Wiederholung den Impuls der ersten Tat und gewinnt zugleich in der Erkenntnis des Impulses die Verdichtung – eine aufmerksame Verlangsamung der Zustände stellt sich ein. Die Differenz entsteht im Moment der entschiedenen Rückkehr und gelingt nur in der Offenheit des Zulassens, nicht in der antizipierten Ausführung. So erscheint die Wiederkehr als Möglichkeit und nicht als Affirmation.

Auf dem Boden liegen 3 Zeichnungen als beredte Warnung: zu dicht an den Dingen. Zwischen der Leidenschaft der Emotion und dem Bewusstsein überlässt sich der Geist dem Geist oder gewährt dem Körper den Vorzug. Die Dichotomie scheint der Fluch der Unvereinbarkeit der Kräfte. Wer entscheidet über das Scheitern oder den Erfolg oder das Scheitern als Erfolg?

26 The horizon rests peacefully beneath the sky. The broad dark ribbon of wooded mountains encircles the city, at once protecting and confining it. The high stony valley guards its anonymity.

No getting through to the language. The melody of labial nasals, the rhythm of flowing sentences, the occasional one, two or three discernible words, and then, jarring with this Romance vernacular, a Slavonic intonation, unfamiliar, indeterminate, a vein of plaintive melancholy, beautiful and gentle.

On the scene. Myth and utopia. The visibility of the image.

26 Der Horizont liegt friedlich unter dem Himmel. Das breite, dunkle Band der bewaldeten Berge legt sich schützend um die Stadt und gebietet ihr Einhalt. Das steinerne Hochtal wahrt seine Anonymität.

Kein Zugang zur Sprache. Die Melodie der labial nasalen Laute hebt an zum Rhythmus fließender Sätze, dazwischen ein Wort, zwei, drei, klar ableitbar und plötzlich bricht aus dem romanischen Klang eine slawische Intonation, fremd und unbestimmt, ein Gesang von klagender Melancholie, schön und sanft.

Über den Schauplatz. Mythos und Utopie. Die Sichtbarkeit des Bildes.

27 The drawing as a scene, course, plan, diagram – no translation, no valid iconography of abstraction deciphers the notations of the spiritual content or narrates the history of the definition of reality, the representation of the understanding of self, the code of which cannot be deciphered semantically. How is abstraction interpretable, how does socio-political awareness show itself, where does content link up with feeling? Who strings the energy of the image into the socio-political discourse on contemporary art? The fragile state of emotion is governed by exegetes who make the chaos of the scene the place of reference solely within the context of their own understanding, of the applicability of their own theorems, for not until the text is written can it kindle the senses of theory.

The sweat of the early afternoon soaks my forearm, my pencil is sticky, my thighs squeak across the leatherette, theory disintegrates. Pink storm clouds tower above the distant mountains and announce the refreshing breeze that will not come. The drawings, arranged in three groups of accomplished failure, lie in the shelf. The city is proving to be a strong adversary, bides its time, stays still. The apparently 'last' drawing strikes a pompous last chord, a false *allegro furioso*, the flourishing embellishment of an act of self-announcement in a fatal pose.

79 x 160 cm are the measurements of the studio, a charcoal-grey laminated multiplex desktop on which things have been organizing themselves with mutually tolerable neatness, order and precision, and in changing hierarchies, for the past 27 days. The desktop right

27 Die Zeichnung als Schauplatz, Parcours, Plan, Diagramm. Keine Übersetzung, keine gültige Ikonographie des Ungegenständlichen entziffert die Partitur der Seelenkonstruktion oder beschreibt die Geschichte der Definition von Wirklichkeit, Abbild des Ich-Verständnisses, dessen Kodierung nicht semantisch dechiffrierbar ist. Wie wird die Abstraktion lesbar, wie zeigt sich gesellschaftspolitisches Bewusstsein, wo knüpft Inhalt an die Empfindung? Wer ordnet die Energie des Bildes in den politisch-soziologischen Diskurs zur künstlerischen Zeitgenossenschaft? Über den fragilen Zustand der Empfindung herrschen die Exegeten, die dem Chaos des Schauplatzes den Ort der Referenz ausschließlich innerhalb ›ihrer‹ Lesbarkeit zuweisen, die einzig von der Übertragbarkeit der eigenen Theoreme abhängt, denn erst der Text entzündet die Sinne der Theorie.

Der Schweiß des frühen Nachmittags umfängt den Unterarm, der Stift ist klebrig, die Oberschenkel quetschen sich über das Kunstleder, die Theorie löst sich auf. In der Ferne türmen sich rosafarbene Gewitterwolken über den Bergen und künden die erfrischende Eilung an, die nicht kommen wird. In drei Gruppen vollendeten Scheiterns geordnet liegen die Zeichnungen im Regal. Die Stadt erweist sich als starker Gegner, wartet ab, steht still. Die scheinbar ›letzte‹ Zeichnung setzt den pompösen Schlussakkord, ein falsches ›allegro furioso‹, Ornament einer Selbstankündigung mit fataler Pose.

79 x 160 cm misst das Atelier, eine anthrazit beschichtete Multiplexplatte, auf der sich die Bereiche knapp und präzise in tolerierter Ordnung und abweichenden Hierar-

next to the bed is the control center, the constant of the apartment, the place of action high above the city.

The world through the open window. In the mornings and in the evenings cool air ventilates the raised hide, the gathering wind peters out in the room, becomes a mere breath that floats across the desktop, almost imperceptibly, touching the body, soothing it, doing it good. Where am I? No answer above the metallic roar of the breathing city. The occasional barking of a dog, plaintive, demanding, resigned.

The drawings are out of sight. They lie between covers of grey cardboard, collected failure, attempted dialogues, monologues of solitude. Notations, plans, vessels and constructions of the imagination, measures of the state of body and soul. Forty times. Discontinued conversations, exclamations, impulsive annexations of territories.

The disciplines of nothingness. Leaves of the shamans. Collected paths and clearings. The jungle of the city, the endless expanse in the confines of the skull. The space between eye and hand, the body between sleep and sleep.

The dilemma lies in the immanence of the resistance to a monopolization of the artistic message, this for its part being constituted precisely by the fact that its eludes demystification. It is the principle of unequal intensity [Novalis]. Appropriation takes place with a certain delay, and as a result of popularized integration, rather than of any individual affinity of feeling.

The exegetes preserve the order of things. Their measure is the subjective projection curve that yearns

chien seit 27 Tagen organisieren. Der Tisch ist die Zentrale, die Konstante der Behausung neben dem Bett, der Ort der Handlung über der Stadt.

Die Welt bei offenem Fenster. Morgens wie abends umfängt die kühle Luft den Hochsitz, der aufkommende Wind verliert sich im Raum, treibt einen Hauch vor sich her, streift über den Tisch, unmerklich fast, körpernah, lindernd und gut. Wo bin ich hier? Keine Antwort über dem atmenden Lärm, röhrend und spitz. Dazwischen ein Hund, klagend, fordernd, resigniert.

Die Zeichnungen sind unsichtbar. Sie ruhen zwischen Deckeln aus Graupappe, gesammeltes Scheitern, versuchte Zwiesprache, Monologe der Einsamkeit. Partituren, Pläne, Gefäße und Gebäude der Vorstellung, das Vermaßen der Befindlichkeit. Vierzig Mal. Angefangene Gespräche, Ausrufe, impulsive Annexion der Territorien.

Die Disziplinen des Nichts. Blattwerk der Schamanen. Gesammelte Pfade und Lichtungen. Das Dickicht der Stadt, die unendliche Weite in der Enge des Kopfes. Der Raum zwischen Auge und Hand, der Körper zwischen Schlaf und Schlaf.

Das Dilemma besteht in der Immanenz des Widerstandes gegenüber der Vereinnahmung der künstlerischen Aussage, die sich gerade dadurch konstituiert, dass sie sich der Entmystifizierung entzieht. Es ist das Prinzip der ungleichen Intensität [Novalis]. Die Aneignung erfolgt zeitlich versetzt als Resultat populistischer Integration, seltener durch ungewöhnliche Affinität eigenständiger Empfindung.

Die Exegeten wahren die Ordnung der Dinge. Ihr Maß

for confirmation; it is not the exposure that follows feeling, pain and pleasure. The fulfillment of the their own small criteria presupposes the acceptance of the work. Art is silent. The artist goes for a stroll and is colonized.

The night rests beneath the warm reflection of the light from the deeply hanging clouds. The lights of the city shimmer right up to the edge of the mountain range, beyond which nothingness falls into the gulf between the sky and the earth. Later the sky drops into the city, fills the gaps, floods the plain, swallows the contours. No buildings, no verticals in sight, dark retreat.

The pose of the last drawing has been outwitted, the organization of the departure interrupted. The Inspector General sticks to the deadline and deletes the anticipated absence.

ist die subjektive Projektionskurve, die sich nach Deckung sehnt und nicht die Entäußerung, die der Empfindung folgt, Schmerz und Lust. Die Erfüllung der eigenen kleinen Kriterien bedingt die Akzeptanz des Werkes. Die Kunst ist stumm. Der Künstler geht spazieren und wird kolonialisiert.

Die Nacht ruht im warmen Licht der Reflexion auf den tief hängenden Wolken. Am Saum des Gebirges flirren die Lichter der Stadt, dahinter fällt das Nichts in die Kluft zwischen Himmel und Erde. Später stürzt der Himmel in die Stadt, füllt die Lücken, überschwemmt die Ebene, schluckt die Konturen. Keine Häuser, keine Vertikale in Sicht, dunkler Rückzug.

Die Pose der letzten Zeichnung ist überlistet, die vorgenommene Einteilung des Aufbruchs unterbrochen. Der Revisor hält sich an die Frist und tilgt die vorweggenommene Abwesenheit.

28 On the road to Paranapicabia in the eastern sierra of Rio Grande da Serra, overwhelming reality ousts imagined images again and again. The present suppresses the imagination and the past superimposes itself on my gaze as I make my way out of the city. The outskirts have fallen apart. Industrial and commercial ruins, the relics of the supply systems of an earlier time, have crumbled away, their wild decay reclaimed by nature's overgrowth, held together by the makeshift constructions of the favelas. Unwanted debris, scarred earth, sorted rubbish, exploited humanity. Here, in this mapless no man's land, nature and culture die the death of destroyed hope. The forced, withering retreat of nature, scorched by the dry rubble of the city, and the decay of the urban sprawl merge and marry in resigned tolerance and desperate resignation.

Paranapicabia.

Swathes of mist waft into the houses like cobwebs, the dew settles over the village, even my hair catches its drops. The wooden fences of the huts are covered with lichen, ferns sprout from the cracks, the tropical forest creeps into the village, lush and fleshy. The white and pink blossoms of the plants shimmer in the diffused light of the deep mist that drifts through the open doors of the houses, beds itself on the orange table-cloths, dances through the rooms. In the middle of the day the matt glow of the streetlamps shines against an impenetrably cloudy barrier. Hummingbirds and dogs romp about in the village. Within seconds a gust of wind shrouds the whole place in dark smoky grey, the

28 Auf dem Weg nach Paranapiacabia in der östlichen Sierra von Rio Grande da Serra drängt sich immer wieder die überwältigend erdrückende Realität vor die Bilder der Vorstellung. Die Gegenwart treibt die Phantasie in die Enge und die Vergangenheit überlagert den Blick auf dem Weg aus der Stadt. Die Stadtränder fallen in sich zusammen, Industrie- und Handelsruinen lösen sich auf, Versorgungsrelikte einer früheren Zeit, deren wilder Verfall von der Natur überwuchert und durch die provisorischen Abfallkonstruktionen der Favelas zusammen gehalten wird. Zurückgelassener Rest, aufgerissene Erde, sortierter Abfall, geschundenes Leben. Im Niemandsland der konturlosen Grenzen sterben Natur und Kultur den Tod zerstörter Hoffnungen. Der bedrängte Rückzug der welken Natur, versengt durch den trockenen Schutt der Stadt, und der Verfall der städtischen Ausdehnung durchdringen und umschlingen sich in müder Toleranz und trostloser Resignation.

Paranapiacabia.

Nebelschwaden wehen wie Spinnenweben in die Häuser, der schwebende Tau legt sich über das Dorf, selbst das Haar fängt die Tropfen. Die Holzzäune der Hütten sind von Flechten überzogen, Farne wachsen aus den Ritzen, der Urwald schleicht in das Dorf, üppig, fleischig. Weiß und rosa beblütet leuchten die Pflanzen im schemenhaften Licht des tiefen Nebels. Die Schwaden ziehen durch die offenen Türen der Häuser, betten sich auf orangefarbene Tischdecken, wehen tanzend durch die Zimmer. Mitten am Tag strahlt die Straßenbeleuchtung matt in die

forest vanishes behind the milky glass, the houses fade into soft nothingness and the balance is upset.

Later a wild flight by bus along the road that cuts through the Mata to Rio Grande da Serra and then out of nature's thicket back into the Moloch of stone. The senses, weighed down by the hopelessness of the present, guide the hand awkwardly, falteringly.

undurchdringlich wolkige Dichte. Kolibris und Hunde tummeln sich im Dorf. Sekundenschnell hüllt ein Windstoß den gesamten Ort in dunkles Rauchgrau, der Urwald verliert sich hinter dem Milchglas, die Häuser tauchen unter im weichen Nichts und das Gleichgewicht hebt sich auf.

Später mit dem Bus in wilder Flucht durch die Schneise der Mata nach Rio Grande da Serra und aus dem Dickicht der Natur zurück in den steinernen Moloch. Die Sinne, bedrückt von der Last der Ausweglosigkeit der Gegenwart, führen die Hand schwer und zögernd.

29 How do I go on? Everything is grinding to a stand-still, the barriers are closing. Strangely calm, my gaze skims over the valley. A jackdaw circles on a rising current, two helicopters begin the day. Many clouds, and between them sunlight on the houses.

Dull throbbing of the hammers in the Copan Building. The buses start off on the Ipiranga, climb to Praça Roosevelt, and then on to the Consolaçao across the top of the Paulista, down the Rebouças into the Jardim and Pinheiros quarters, where they discharge their load to service the bourgeoisie.

Time creeps by at breakneck speed, the desk waits patiently for the daily ritual, the prospect of endless repetition. I decide to quit. Clear up, leave the apartment, climb down from my raised hide on the 28th floor and leave town. Back to Europe. Two drawings lie on the floor next to the desk, begun in brave resistance to my planned departure.

29 Wie mache ich weiter? Alles gerät ins Stocken, die Barrieren schließen sich. Seltsam gleichmütig streift der Blick über das Tal. Eine Dohle kreist im Aufwind, zwei Hubschrauber beginnen den Tag, viel Gewölk, dazwischen Sonne auf den Häusern.

Dumpf pocht der Rhythmus der Hämmer im Copan. Die Omnibusse starten auf der Ipiranga hoch zur Praça Roosevelt, dann auf die Consolação über den Scheitelpunkt der Paulista hinweg und die Rebouças hinunter in die Viertel Jardim und Pinheiros, wo sie sich für den Dienst der Bürger entladen.

Rasend schleicht die Zeit, geduldig wartet der Schreibtisch auf das Ritual der Arbeit, endlos ist die Perspektive der Wiederholungen. Ich entscheide mich für den Abbruch. Aufräumen, das Apartment verlassen, vom Hochsitz des 28. Stockwerkes herabsteigen und aus der Stadt fahren. Zurück nach Europa. Zwei Zeichnungen liegen auf dem Boden neben dem Schreibtisch, angefangen in mutigem Widerstand zum geplanten Aufbruch.

Marcelo Mattos Araújo, São Paulo
Joachim Bernauer, São Paulo
John Brogden, Dortmund
Rein Ergo, Gent / Ghent
Boudi Eskens / Milco Onrust, Amsterdam
Laymert Garcia dos Santos, São Paulo
Owen Griffith, London
Nina / Miriam Lambert, Düsseldorf
Oscar Niemeyer, Rio de Janeiro
Ligia Nobre, São Paulo
Annette Partenheimer, München / Munich
Petra / Klaus-Werner Richter, Düsseldorf
Klaus Schrenk, Karlsruhe
Jan Thorn-Prikker, Bonn

Das Buch erscheint zur Ausstellung
This book is published on the
occasion of the exhibition
Jürgen Partenheimer
Roma – São Paulo.
Zeichnungen / Drawings

Staatliche Kunsthalle Karlsruhe
8.4. – 9. 7. 2006

Pinacoteca do Estado de São Paulo
10.3. – 22.4. 2007

Nietzsche-Haus Sils-Maria
19.7. – 20.10. 2007

Abbildungen / Illustrations

São Paulo 1. [XI] 29-03-05
29 x 19 cm, 2005 (Detail) S./p. 02

São Paulo 1. [V] 28-03-05
29 x 19 cm, 2005 (Detail) S./p. 06

Erstauflage 800 Exemplare sowie
1 Vorzugsausgabe signiert und
numeriert von 15 Exemplaren

First edition 800 copies with a
special edition of 15 signed and
numbered copies

Herausgegeben von / Published by
Staatliche Kunsthalle Karlsruhe
Hans-Thoma-Straße 2-6
76133 Karlsruhe
Direktor: Prof. Dr. Klaus Schrenk

Übersetzung Deutsch – Englisch
Translation German – English
John Brogden, Dortmund

Fotografie / Photography
Wolfgang Grümer, Bruch

Gestaltung / Design
Lambert und Lambert, Düsseldorf

Gesamtherstellung / Production
Heinrich Winterscheidt GmbH,
Düsseldorf

Bibliografische Information
Der Deutschen Bibliothek
*Die Deutsche Bibliothek verzeichnet
diese Publikation in der deutschen
Nationalbibliografie; detaillierte
bibliografische Daten sind im Internet
über http//dnb.ddb.de abrufbar.*

Bibliographic information published by Die Deutsche Bibliothek
*Die Deutsche Bibliothek lists this
publication in the Deutsche
Nationalbibliografie; detailed
bibliographic data are available in
the internet at http://dnb.ddb.de.*

© 2006
Staatliche Kunsthalle Karlsruhe
Jürgen Partenheimer

© der Werke / All works of
Jürgen Partenheimer
VG Bild-Kunst, Bonn 2006

Museumsausgabe / Museum edition
Staatliche Kunsthalle Karlsruhe
ISBN 3-925212-65-5